# handmade books
## *at home*

A Beginner's Guide to Binding Journals, Sketchbooks,
Photo Albums and More

*Chanel Ly*

Creator of
Bitter Melon Bindery

PAGE STREET
PUBLISHING CO.

PAGE STREET
PUBLISHING CO.

First published in 2023 by
Page Street Publishing Co.
27 Congress Street, Suite 1511
Salem, MA 01970
www.pagestreetpublishing.com

Distributed by Macmillan, sales in Canada by The Canadian Manda Group.

27   26   25   24   23     1   2   3   4   5

ISBN-13: 978-1-64567-830-4
ISBN-10: 1-64567-830-X

Library of Congress Control Number: 2022952195

Cover and book design by Meg Baskis for Page Street Publishing Co.
Photography by Lexus Gallegos
Cover photo and Step-by-Step images by Chanel Ly

Printed and bound in the United States of America

# Dedication

To my fellow paper lovers

# Contents

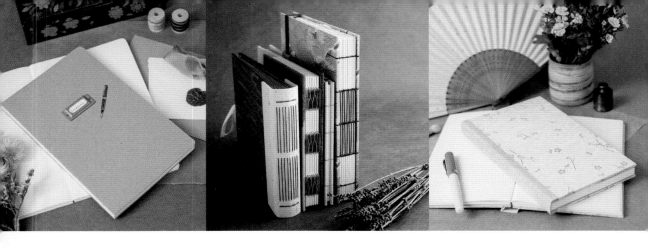

# introduction

------------------------------------------------------------

Crafting books with your own hands is a special experience. Handmade books are one-of-a-kind vessels that will go on to live a life of their own, collecting memories, ideas and countless other possibilities. The art of bookbinding is an old and wondrous world to step into, and I'm thrilled to guide you along your journey. I hope immersing yourself in the process will help you slow down and find moments of presence and peace.

Bookbinding grants you the ability to create a book exactly how you want, especially for a specific purpose. Perhaps you want a journal that you can both write and paint in or a photo album that has covers made with a sentimental cloth. Take delight in making crisp folds, sewing through paper and playing with the textures and prints of handmade papers from around the world. The nature of the craft requires you to take your time and be methodical, and the learning is satisfying every step of the way.

After making my first book in 2013, I found myself swept up by the magic of bookbinding. I loved paper, stationery and writing everything down by hand, so it was clear to me that I had to make my own journals. I made many scrappy, wonky books in the beginning, and although they were not Instagram-friendly, I found a deep satisfaction in the discovery process. I started Bitter Melon Bindery to fund my beloved hobby, selling books at craft markets and refining my skills and style. When I was burnt out from my non-profit job in 2020, I turned to bookbinding for comfort. It was then when I decided to pick up my camera and share photos and videos of my process online. Sharing my bookbinding experience and knowledge became an unexpected new passion.

By combining modern and traditional methods, you'll understand the intricacies of working with paper and making books that will last beyond a lifetime. The projects included in this book focus on stationery binding (versus letterpress binding), which allows you to create books with blank pages for a wide range of uses. Stationery bindings need structures that are built to withstand use and support ample movement and flexibility. In this book, I will share all the tools, materials and techniques you need to make beautiful books at home. Let's get started!

Happy bookbinding,

# book anatomy

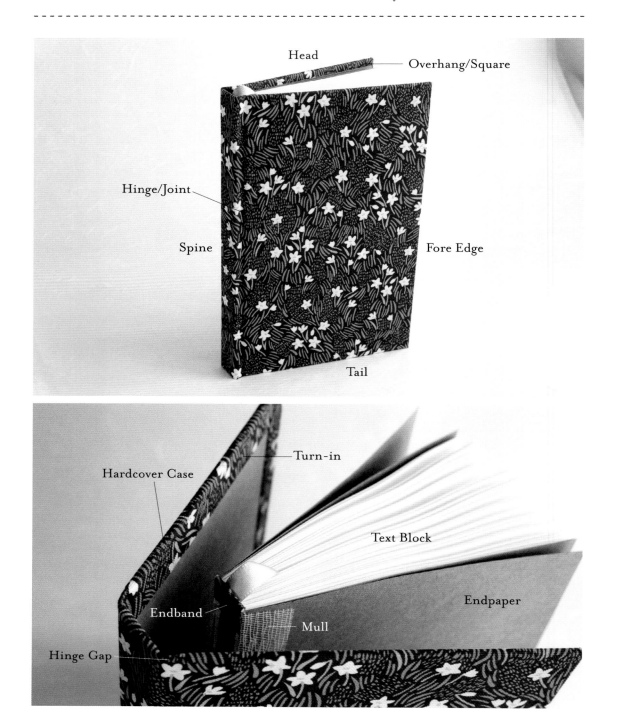

Head

Overhang/Square

Hinge/Joint

Spine

Fore Edge

Tail

Turn-in

Hardcover Case

Text Block

Endband

Endpaper

Mull

Hinge Gap

# gather your personal toolkit

## A Beginner's Checklist

- Utility knife
- Scissors
- Metal ruler
- Cutting mat
- Bone folder
- Awl
- Bookbinding needles
- Glue brush
- Book pressing tools
- Other useful tools

## Blades for Every Application

An 18-mm utility knife with snap-off blades is the tool I pick up the most for cutting all types of paper. It's suitable for cutting book board and medium-weight to heavyweight papers, as well as hand-trimming text blocks. A smaller blade, such as a 9-mm utility knife or a precision knife, can be used for light duty jobs, curves and finer cuts.

For book cloth and delicate papers, a rotary cutter works well. It makes straight cuts quickly and is gentler on lightweight papers. Whichever blade you use, be sure to make your cuts on a cutting mat (see next page) to protect your tabletop.

Good scissors are indispensable. I have a few pairs: one that is multi-purpose, one for fabric and a small pair for cutting thread. Fabric shears typically have sharper blades. Avoid using fabric shears to cut paper, as paper is more abrasive than fabric and can quickly dull the blades.

*Starter recommendation: 18-mm utility knife and multi-purpose scissors*

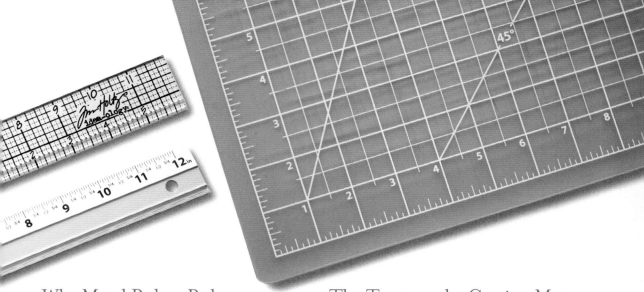

## Why Metal Rulers Rule

Rulers are used for cutting as much as measuring, given that cutting straight edges is a regular occurrence. The most common cutting method is anchoring a ruler on the paper and gliding a blade along the ruler edge to achieve a clean, straight cut. Since the blade runs along the edge of the ruler, the ruler material needs to be durable. Start with a ruler with a non-slip backing to prevent accidental slipping. Non-slip stainless steel rulers are commonly found at local arts and crafts stores. A metal ruler is also excellent for tearing heavyweight paper to achieve soft edges. I prefer to use rulers with hatch marks of both imperial and metric measurement systems on either side.

*Starter recommendation: non-slip stainless steel ruler at least 15 inches (38 cm) long*

**Ruler type tips:** Look for non-slip rulers that sit flat on the surface and have a raised edge to protect fingers from stray blades. Clear rulers with a grid allow you to easily draw square lines. Use a 90 degree triangle or L-square to draw and check for square corners.

## The Trustworthy Cutting Mat

I enjoy working on a large self-healing cutting mat (24 x 36 inches [61 x 91 cm]) that covers the majority of my desk so I can make long cuts without damaging the tabletop. Cutting mats come in different colors and sizes and are easy to wipe clean. I use the grid lines regularly to make quick measurements and square cuts. I have a smaller, portable cutting mat (12 x 18 inches [30.5 x 45.7 cm]) for specific jobs like trimming text blocks (see page 25 for technique).

*Starter recommendation: cutting mat at least 12 x 18 inches (30.5 x 45.7 cm) with ½-inch or centimeter grid lines (or the largest mat size your space allows)*

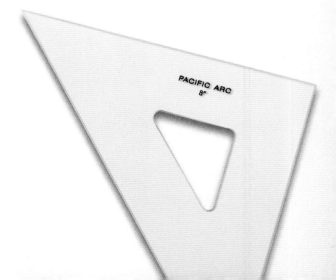

## Bone Folders and Vegan Alternatives

Paper folders are made of a hard, smooth material that won't make marks on the paper surface. The purposes of the tool are to crease sharp, clean folds, to score paper and to smooth out glued material. The standard design has a tapered tip for scoring and reaching small spaces. Folders are tradition-ally made of bovine bone, but if you want a vegan alternative, look for Teflon™, plastic or agate folders. I find that a folder about 6 inches (15.2 cm) long and ⅞ inch (2.2 cm) wide feels the most comfortable in my hands.

*Starter recommendation: standard size bone folder (tapered on one end and rounded on the other end)*

## Bookbinder's Awl (or "That Pointy Tool")

In bookbinding, holes are punched into cover boards and signatures (folded sections of the book) in preparation for sewing. Since the holes only need to be wide enough for the sewing needle and thread to pass through, look for an awl with a strong, straight and thin needle. The handle should feel comfortable in your hand to hold. Avoid light duty awls and tapered awls. Light duty awls typically have needles that can bend and break, and tapered awls are used for enlarging holes. Holes that are too big can cause loose, uneven sewing and let glue seep through the folds into the pages.

*Starter recommendation: standard bookbinding or paper awl with a straight needle and your preferred handle*

## My Favorite Type of Needle

I prefer using 2-inch (5-cm) curved needles for all my sewing. The curve of the needle allows for a better grip when sewing through tight spaces and easier maneuvering between signatures in bindings such as Coptic Stitch (page 94) and French Link Stitch (page 46). A straight needle, however, is great for Japanese Stab Binding (page 70).

Many bookbinders use straight needles with blunt tips since the holes are pre-punched. Blunt tips also mean that fingers are less likely to get pricked. Straight needles with #18 gauge is a common thickness, but you can use any needle that is no thicker than the needle of the awl and can pass through punched holes without enlarging them substantially.

*Starter recommendation: 2-inch (5-cm) curved needle or #18 gauge straight needle multi-pack (in case you lose or break one)*

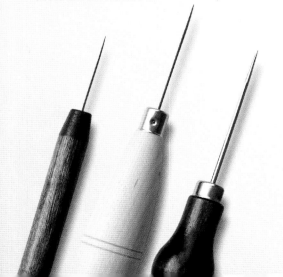

## Best Brushes for Gluing

Bristle brushes work great for gluing, and there are many suitable options for bookbinding. Small or flat brushes are ideal for narrow areas such as turn-ins, and round or wide brushes can pick up a generous amount of glue for larger areas, such as covering boards or pasting endpapers. It's important to use sturdy brushes that can be washed repeatedly. Brushes with longer bristles (over 1 inch [2.5 cm]) tend to last longer because glue is less likely to creep up towards the handle where it's more difficult to rinse out.

In my early years of bookbinding, I used foam brushes for gluing. I like the even application of foam, as they soak up excess glue like a sponge. Foam brushes are readily available at the arts and crafts store and are a good option for beginners. However, foam brushes are not as environmentally friendly because they are more disposable than bristle brushes.

**Brush care tips:** Before each use, dry brush your hand to remove dust and loose bristles. We'll be using PVA glue, which is water soluble and easy to clean from your brushes. Simply rinse the brushes when you're done, squeeze out the excess water, and let dry. If glue has started to set into the bristles, you can soak them in warm water for a few hours.

*Starter recommendation: flat bristle or foam brush 1 inch (2.5 cm) wide*

## Press to Impress

Bookbinders commonly use an advanced tool called a book press. They are handy for flattening book components, creating compact text blocks (sewn blocks of pages), and finishing books. Pressing sets the glue and papers together so that the finished book will dry flat and compressed. I made a book press for my own practice, and you can find the instructions on page 186.

Before committing to buying or making a book press, there are a few easy alternatives to try. For pressing text blocks, I recommend starting with two C-clamps or ratchet spring clamps with deep throats from the hardware store.

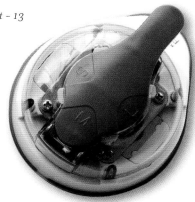

Use wood pressing boards with weights for light to medium pressing power. Pressing boards can also be used to apply light uniform weight to flatten components, such as signatures and cover boards. Find boards that are solid, flat, and warp resistant. Quality plywood with a clear protective finish is an ideal material.

I purchased a large sheet of 2 x 2–feet (61 x 61–cm) plywood that was cut into quarters at the hardware store. I sanded it smooth and applied a natural stain and clear finish. They have been very useful in my workflow!

## Other Useful Tools

Here are some other tools that are mentioned in the projects that you may want to add to your personal toolkit.

A **pencil and eraser** are essential for drawing cut lines and guide lines for positioning materials. Sharpen your pencil regularly for more accurate markings.

**Clips** can be useful for holding signatures together while sewing, especially for thin and soft cover books. I look for clips that have a strong hold and are least likely to make impressions in the paper. You can use stationery clips, such as binder clips or bulldog clips.

**Fine-grit sandpaper**, such as 220 grit, is helpful for smoothing book board and text block edges. Whether you are trimming text blocks by hand or with a guillotine, there may be visible marks or rough spots left by the blade. Be sure to firmly press the text block edges before sanding.

**Weights** are used in various stages of bookbinding to press and flatten book components. It's best to place a large, flat, rigid board (made of any material) directly on top of your work, then add weights on top. Large heavy books are a popular choice. You can also use bricks wrapped in kraft paper.

A **corner rounder** provides a practical and charming way to finish soft cover books and prevent page corners from becoming dog-eared. There are handheld corner rounders that can round a few sheets at a time. Use an industrial corner rounder to round more sheets at once.

A **scoring tool** can help make folds more precise. Scoring heavier weight paper before folding can create crisper folds. It can also help create clean hinges on softcover notebooks.

# choosing quality materials

- - - - - - - - - - - - - - - - - - - - - - - - - - - - - - - - - - - - - - - - - - - - - - - - - - - - -

## A Beginner's Checklist

- Text block paper
- Decorative paper
- Book board
- Glue
- Gluing materials
- Thread
- Spine supports and linings
- Book cloth
- Endbands

## Paper for Pages

The first question to ask yourself is, what will the book be used for? After deciding the purpose of the book, consider the paper type and weight. You can use virtually any paper for the pages, but you may want to source a quality paper that offers a pleasant experience when using your favorite pen or medium.

When I'm at the art supply store, I look for loose-leaf reams or glue-bound sketch paper pads, where each sheet can be easily removed to fold into signatures. The cardboard backings of sketch pads can also be repurposed as book board. For wire-bound sketchbooks, you can cut the paper into loose sheets and recycle the wire.

Stationery papers designed for writing with various types of pens and inks are difficult to find in loose-leaf reams, as office supply stores rarely sell them. I purchase all my journal papers online by searching the desired paper type and weight. Every paper is manufactured differently. If possible, order samples to test the color, finish and quality before committing to a larger order.

In North America, paper with 60 to 80lb text weight or 24 to 32lb writing weight (both equivalent to 90 to 120gsm) is suitable for use in notebooks and journals. Look for papers that are marketed as stationery papers, as well as papers that are popular among other bookbinders, journalers and fountain pen users.

## Suggested Paper Weights and Sheets per Signature*

| Journals | 60–80lb text weight (90–120gsm) | 4–6 sheets per signature |
|---|---|---|
| Mix media sketchbooks | 160–190gsm** | 3–5 sheets per signature |
| Watercolor sketchbooks | 185–640gsm** | 1–2 sheets per signature |
| Photo albums and scrapbooks | 80–100lb cover weight (216–270gsm) | 2 sheets per signature |

*The number of sheets per signature can be adjusted in consideration of book structure, spine swell (page 181) and how readily the pages turn.

**Visual art paper brands use different labels to mark paper weight, so I've only listed the grams per square meter (gsm) weight here, which is the most consistent and reliable.

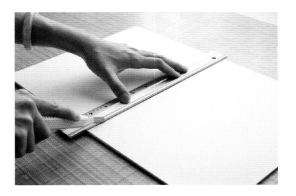

Card stock or cover weight paper is a multi-purpose material. It's a stiff, heavy-weight paper typically used as soft covers, endpapers, sturdy pages for albums or as a spine stiffener. The most common weights are 80 to 100lb (216 to 270gsm) cover weight. In North America, they are typically available in letter size (8½ x 11 inches [21.6 x 27.9 cm]) and 12 x 12 inches (30.5 x 30.5 cm). I love going to the arts and crafts store to check out their patterned and textured card stock supply.

Letter paper (8½ x 11 inches [21.6 x 27.9 cm]) is the most common paper size in North America, but it always has the grain running lengthwise (long grain). Since I'm usually looking to fold letter paper from short edge to short edge (AKA hamburger style) to make an A5 journal, the paper grain needs to run widthwise (short grain). For this reason, I source reams of paper that measure 11 x 17 inches (27.9 x 43.2 cm) that I cut in half to achieve the proper grain for the signatures. For art paper, every brand and sketch pad has a different grain so I recommend looking at the papers in-store. Go to page 20 for more information about identifying paper grain.

You may want to make notebooks and journals with lines, dots or other layouts. One option is to get it printed at your local printer for best results. Be sure to do test prints and talk to the printer about achieving the correct paper grain. You can also print at home with a template found for free or cheap online. For some common spacing measurements, college ruled paper has horizontal lines spaced $9/32$ inch (7.1 mm) apart, and dot grids are typically spaced $3/16$ inch (5 mm) apart. I've had mixed results with printing dot grids depending on the printer and paper type, so be sure to test your prints before producing a full journal's worth!

> Tip: Look for papers labeled "acid-free," "pH neutral," or "archival quality." Acidic paper will turn yellow and become brittle over time, which significantly shortens the life of the paper. Acidic paper can last about one lifetime, ranging from 50 to 100 years, while non-acidic paper can last much longer with proper storage and care.

## Decorative Papers, My Greatest Weakness

Immersing myself in the world of handmade, traditional papers from around the world is a major reason why I still make books today. The rich cultural histories and community-based production methods made me more curious about paper making. I was delighted to learn that many commercially available handmade papers are tree-free, often made from quick-growing bushes that are indigenous to the land of origin. Here are a few types that I always keep handy in my studio:

**Lokta paper** (image A) is handmade with the stems of lokta bushes that grow wildly and abundantly in the Himalayan forests in Nepal. Historically, lokta paper was used for Buddhist and government texts. Today, it's used for many forms of paper craft all over the world. Lokta paper comes in sheets of about 20 x 30 inches (51 x 76 cm) and in many beautiful bold colors and patterns. The standard weight is 45 to 60gsm, but it comes in heavier weights as well. They're a preferred paper among bookbinders to use as endpapers because they don't have a distinct paper grain, so they're more forgiving when glued.

**Chiyogami paper** (image B) is a type of washi that is machine made and silkscreened by hand in Japan. The papers feature stunning traditional Japanese patterns that are inspired by kimono textiles. They were traditionally printed with woodblocks and used to make paper dolls and decorate tea tins and small boxes. Chiyogami papers are very strong and come in large sheets (24 x 36 inches [61 x 91 cm]) with a weight of 47lb (70gsm), so they make wonderful book covers.

**Marbled papers** were developed in Japan in the 12th century, where the practice is called *Suminagashi*, meaning "ink floating." Then in the 15th century, a practice called *Ebru*, meaning "cloud art," was developed in Turkey using heavier paints. Marbling eventually spread across Europe and is now a modern art practiced by many. Hand-marbled papers are generally durable enough to use as book covers, and they make beautiful accents as endpapers. The paper types and weights used for marbling can vary depending on the preference of the marbling artist.

**Washi** literally translates to "Japanese paper." Washi encompasses both handmade and machine-made papers created from mulberry (kozo), gampi, and mitsumata plants. Within bookbinding, washi is used for both structural and aesthetic purposes. It's known for being very thin yet having a lot of strength, so thinner tissue papers are often used as spine linings and backing book cloth, among other purposes.

Decorative, handmade papers are an excellent choice for endpapers, which are attached to the inner covers at the beginning and end of the book. These papers are reliably high quality, which typically means that they can handle glue well. Choosing endpapers is a fun, creative opportunity to add color and personality to the inside of the book.

Alternatively, quality patterned papers and art papers found at the arts and crafts store are wonderful options for endpapers as well. A popular art paper among bookbinders is the Canson Mi-Teintes®.

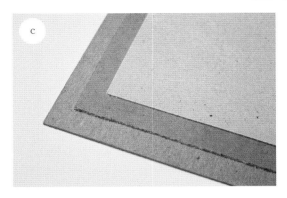

## Book Board for Every Hard Cover

**Book board** (image C) is the material used to create the front and back covers of a book. Also known as binders board, book board is a dense, thick cardboard made of raw or recycled wood pulp. Thickness is labeled in decimals and typically ranges from 0.059 to 0.120 inches (1.5 to 3 mm). Sourcing board that is manufactured for bookbinding is ideal, since they're guaranteed to be acid-free and designed to resist warping. Types of book board include Davey Board, archival grey board and mill board. However, these can be difficult to find depending on your location.

Alternative options for book board can be found at your local art supply or craft store. **Museum, mount and mat boards used for framing** are acid-free and come in various neutral colors. They're typically thinner and less dense than book board. **Chipboard** is an excellent budget-friendly and recycled option that I used for many years. It comes in different thicknesses and ranges in quality, depending on the source. Chipboard may not be acid-free, but they are great for making journals and sketchbooks.

For standard-sized books, I recommend starting with a 0.08 inch (2 mm) board thickness. Experiment with a thinner or thicker board depending on the size and aesthetic of the book project. Generally, you can increase the thickness of the boards for larger books.

If acid-free isn't a priority, feel free to use anything for the covers! For example, you can repurpose the backs of sketch paper pads, flat canvases, old book covers, used notebook covers, even board game boxes.

## Glues for Structure and Flexibility

Glue is the unsung hero of bookbinding. It holds everything together to help the book withstand a lifetime of use. The most commonly used glue is archival quality PVA (polyvinyl acetate), which is non-toxic and becomes clear and flexible once dried. PVA glue can lose adhesion if it's been frozen, so purchase glue during the warmer months if ordering online.

In a pinch, you can use white craft glue available at the arts and crafts store. Look for an "acid-free" or "pH-neutral" label where possible, as acidic glue can become brittle over time and cause paper to yellow. Glue sticks offer a low-moisture option, but I would only recommend them as a backup and for temporary adhesion. Glue sticks can also dry brittle and lose their adhesion over a short time.

Wheat paste and methyl cellulose are plant-based glues, which are typically mixed in with PVA to extend the drying time for advanced bindings. They have a much shorter shelf life than PVA. Using wheat paste or methyl cellulose is not necessary as a beginner, but it might be of interest when you graduate to more complex bindings.

Note: Sticky tapes like repair tape, hinge tape and double-sided tape are typically used for quick repairs and simple bindings. Feel free to try them in your practice for extra support.

## Necessities for a Successful Gluing Job

Here are some other materials that are mentioned in the projects that can make it easier to glue cleanly and efficiently.

**Waste sheets and boards** are ideal for covering your workspace and masking for gluing. Collect clean scrap papers for this. For each book that involves gluing, have at least one large sheet and a few medium sheets of paper on hand. Sturdy waste sheets can be reused many times. Keep scrap book boards and sketch pad backings to use as pressing boards for gluing and lining text block spines. Use clear tape along the board edges to prevent the text block and boards from sticking to each other.

**Moisture barriers** are typically used at the end of the bookbinding process. The finished project is set to dry with a moisture barrier sheet placed in between the glued endpapers and the text block to protect the papers from moisture. A common material to use is wax paper. Other materials that bookbinders use are acetate, mylar or thin metal sheets. You can also use an absorbent material, such as blotting and watercolor paper.

**Rubbing sheets**, like parchment or vellum paper, are helpful when pasting decorative papers or endpapers. The freshly glued paper might be vulnerable to bunching or tearing from rubbing with your hand or bone folder. To protect the papers, you can place a thin sheet of parchment or vellum paper under the bone folder as you smooth it out.

A **jar of water and wet cloth** can keep things clean and save you time. Working with glue can get messy quickly, and you may not have time to make trips to the sink to rinse your brush or wash your hands. Having a jar of water on your desk can help keep your brush wet, as dried glue can render your brush useless. A wet cloth can help you wipe your hands clean in between gluing different parts of the book. Sticky, gluey fingers can be dangerous in proximity to precious papers and materials!

## Thread—Why Waxed Linen is Best

Thread made of linen is most preferred by bookbinders because of its strength. Linen thread comes in various gauges (smaller number means thicker) and plies (number of strands). I recommend starting with a medium thread ($^{18}/_3$) for exposed spine bindings, and a thin thread ($^{25}/_3$) to sew text blocks for case bindings. Consider how the thread will affect the spine swell, which is the increased thickness of the spine after the signatures are sewn (page 181).

Coating thread with wax ensures that it doesn't fray when it's pulled through paper. It is less likely to tangle, and the threads have more grip to hold signatures and covers together. I often use pre-waxed threads that come in a variety of colors, which are excellent for exposed spine books. You can wax your own thread by pulling a pre-measured thread through a block of beeswax a few times (image D). If you don't have access to beeswax or prefer to not use it, candles are a backup option for waxing thread. Wax the thread just enough without adding bulk or extra stickiness. You may also opt to leave the thread unwaxed if you feel like it's strong enough.

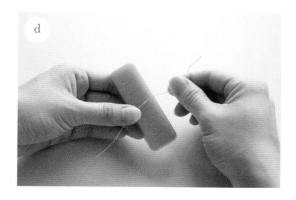

Alternative threads that you can use for sewing are nylon or polyester thread, thin beading cord and embroidery floss. Sewing with these threads can vary in results. It's important to source thread that is strong and does not stretch.

## Spine Supports and Linings that Last

For hardcover books with flat or round backs, the text block spine is glued and lined after it is sewn. A well-supported spine can sustain a wide range of movement while staying intact. The spine linings and any other sewing supports are wider than the spine and are affixed onto the inner covers, supporting the hinges as well.

The first layer of support applied with glue is mull (image E), a stiffened, open-weave cotton or linen cloth. The open weave offers a strong and flexible hold when it's glued. Mull is also known as super or crash. An alternative to mull that I have used is unbleached 90-grade cheesecloth.

Another layer that can be added for extra reinforcement is Japanese tissue paper, which is incredibly strong for its light weight. It's a preferred material because it doesn't add any bulk to the spine. Source any type of Japanese tissue paper with a smooth finish and a weight of around 30gsm or less. Japanese tissue paper is often made of long kozo fibers ("kozo" is also known as mulberry), which has a strong hold when glued.

Thick heavy books need even more support, so text blocks are sewn with tapes or cords before the linings are applied. These added materials are called sewing supports, which are also attached to the inner covers, helping the book open with less stress on the signatures. Supported sewing structures are considered more advanced. You can experiment with additional supports as you graduate to making larger books with more pages. The sewing process in Long Stitch with Cloth Tapes (page 82) is one method of supported sewing for text blocks. For small- to medium-sized books, the French Link Stitch (page 46) offers adequate support.

Upgrade Your Toolbox: If you plan to make many future text blocks with supported sewing, such as with tapes or cords, a sewing frame may be helpful. The sewing frame holds tapes and cords vertically with tension so that the binder can sew the text block comfortably.

## Book Cloth and Endbands

Book cloth and endbands can be purchased from online bookbinding supply shops. Commercial book cloth is reliably high quality, wear-resistant and designed to last on library shelves. Book cloth has a built-in moisture barrier and is paper-backed so that it can be glued to book board. Look for tutorials online to make your own book cloth out of fabric. To learn more about endbands, go to page 137.

# techniques to build your skills

## Recognizing Paper Grain

Paper grain is the direction that the pulp fibers are arranged in the manufacturing process, running lengthwise or widthwise on a sheet of paper. Letter size paper, the most common paper size in North America, always has the grain running lengthwise, meaning that the paper is long grain.

**Grain long**: grain direction runs along the length of the paper sheet

**Grain short**: grain direction runs along the width of the paper sheet

When sheets of paper are folded along the grain, as opposed to against the grain (cross grain), there is less stress on the folds, allowing for smoother, crisper folds. This is a major reason why paper grain in books needs to run head to tail (parallel to the spine). Books that have the correct grain direction can open more readily and have pages that turn more smoothly.

Note: When heavier weight papers are folded against the grain, cracking can occur at the fold.

### Identifying Paper Grain

1. Take a close look at the surface of the paper. You may be able to see the direction that the paper fibers are arranged.

2. Bend the paper vertically, then horizontally. One direction should feel like it bends with more ease. The paper grain runs along that bend, the direction in which it will fold easier. For lighter papers, pinch the paper to feel for the direction with least resistance. If it's difficult to tell, fold the paper and find the direction that results in a flatter, crisper fold.

3. Tear the paper, at least a few inches, vertically. Then tear the paper horizontally. The direction that the paper tears in a straighter line is the paper grain. In the example below, the vertical tear was much cleaner, showing this paper's grain runs lengthwise.

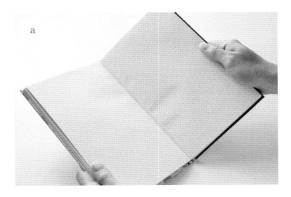

Once you've identified the grain of papers for your book project, note it by drawing an arrow pointing up toward the head of the book. This will be a helpful reference during the binding process.

> Note: Many handmade papers don't have a distinct paper grain, as pulp fibers settle randomly on the paper mold.

Paper grain is also important for understanding paper expansion and contraction. When moisture is introduced to paper, the fibers expand across the grain. Each type of paper will expand different amounts. It's easier to predict and control the amount of expansion and paper pull on the boards when the grain of all the papers and board are running in the same direction.

Besides glue, environmental factors like humidity can cause paper to expand and contract. When books are bound with cross grain paper, pages can ripple along the gutter from the fibers expanding along the spine (image A). This does not affect the functionality of the book, but it will be noticeable. I've made many books with cross grain paper, and I've found that I have better results with structures that require little to no glue, such as single signature and exposed spine bindings. You may choose to make cross grain books if access to sourcing paper is limited, or there's a specific piece of board or decorative paper you want to use.

## Making Covers that Stay Flat

Bowing boards was a consistent, perplexing issue I faced in my beginning years of bookbinding (and sometimes still do). It took me a while to understand that this is normal and expected when a cover material is applied onto book board with glue, which creates a pulling effect from paper expanding and contracting.

The general rule to prevent covers from warping and bowing is to use a similar type of paper on both sides of the board so that the paper pull is balanced. When you start using different materials, you can experiment with various types and weights of paper to understand their pulling force. Thicker papers like card stock have the least amount of pull (expands the least), and thinner papers like Japanese tissue have the most amount of pull (expands the most). Book board manufactured for bookbinding, such as Davey board, has built-in warp resistance, so it's more forgiving to moisture. It's also important to ensure the grain of the papers and board run in the same direction, parallel to the spine.

It's best practice to let covers and cases dry completely before pasting the endpapers. This way, you'll more likely be able to predict the final result. For hardcover cases, it's acceptable for the boards to bow slightly outward. When the endpapers are pasted onto the inner covers and the book is pressed, the covers should be pulled inward and flattened.

> Note: Larger covers are more likely to bow than smaller covers.

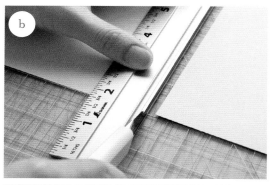

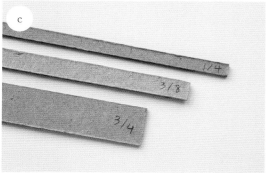

## Making Square Cuts

Books will look and function their best when all of their parts are square. Tools like the L-square, T-square and 90-degree triangle rulers can be used to draw cut lines and check corners. A simple card cut with 90-degree angles can also be used as a guide for checking square lines and angles. I like to follow the grid lines of the cutting mat to make quick cuts (image B).

An easy method to make square cuts and measurements is to use spacers (image C). You can make your own with book board. I often use my ¾ inch (1.9 cm) spacer for trimming the turn-ins, where decorative material is wrapped around the book board edges. I use ¼- or ⅜-inch (6- or 10-mm) spacers for the hinge gaps when making hardcover cases.

## Mindful Gluing

Gluing results are best when it's done mindfully and decisively. I've lost precious material from gluing mistakes. This loss is part of the learning process! As you work with different types of papers, you'll learn how each one reacts to glue and moisture. Drying times also vary depending on your location and the weather (namely temperature and humidity). With practice and experience, I'm confident you'll become very familiar with using glue.

Here are some gluing pro tips:

1. Use a brush size that is proportional to the size of your work.

2. The glue should be spreadable into a thin film, with a consistency between honey and maple syrup.

3. Dip your brush into a glue container or use a squeeze bottle to control the amount of glue used. When there's too little glue, there's a risk of papers drying too quickly and causing air bubbles when the material is attached. With too much glue, papers are more likely to wrinkle or tear because they're too wet.

4. Plan out your gluing steps and be prepared with waste sheets and moisture barrier sheets for smooth transitions to next stages.

5. Brush from the center of the paper moving outward (image D), with gentle pressure. The friction of the brush on the paper can pull the paper fibers. Also, paper will expand with moisture, so this will help it expand more evenly.

6. It's inevitable that you're going to get glue all over your fingers! Wash or wipe your hands often so you don't accidentally get glue residue on your cover or pages, which is very difficult to remove.

## The Ins and Outs of Sewing Knots

Here are the basic knots you need to know for sewing text blocks:

**Overhand knots** are used for starting the sewing process. Tie the overhand knot twice for extra bulk to prevent thread ends from slipping through holes.

• To tie the overhand knot, create a loop, and thread the working end through the loop (image E). Pull to tighten.

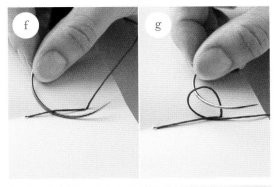

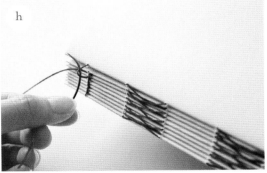

The **half hitch knot** is a tidy way to finish and secure the sewing on the inside of the book.

• To tie the half hitch knot, make sure your thread is on the inside of a signature. Thread the needle under a stitch (image F) to create a loop and thread the working end through the loop (image G). Pull in the direction of sewing, away from the stitches to tighten. You can tie another knot over the first one for extra support.

**Kettle stitches** are sewn at the end of each row of the text block to lock the signatures together.

• To sew the kettle stitch, sew behind the stitch of the previous signature and pull to create a small loop. Sew up through the loop and pull taut (image H). Avoid over-tightening kettle stitches to achieve proper thread tension.

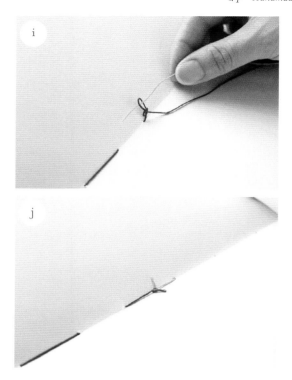

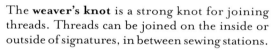

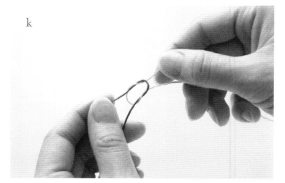

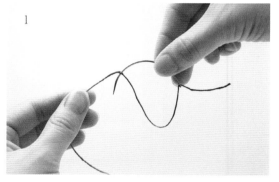

The **weaver's knot** is a strong knot for joining threads. Threads can be joined on the inside or outside of signatures, in between sewing stations.

• To tie the weaver's knot, start by making a slip knot with the remaining working thread (red) in the signature. Tie a slip knot by creating a loop and passing a U-shape through the loop with the working thread. Pass the end of the new thread (yellow) through the loop (image I) and pull the end of the slip knot to close the loop around the new thread. Pull the old and new thread ends to lock the knot. Then trim their ends (image J). If the knot slips, re-tie the weaver's knot. This can take a few tries.

A **reef knot** is an alternative knot to join threads. It's not as strong as the weaver's knot, but it is easier to tie.

• To tie the reef knot, tie two thread ends together (image K), and then tie the ends one more time. Pull both ends to tighten.

You may want to **secure the thread** onto the needle while you sew, to prevent the thread from slipping out.

• With the needle threaded, pierce the working thread (image L), about a few inches down, and pull the needle through. Then pull the working thread to close the loop. Press the thread to flatten.

The project instructions will refer to these knots for various stages of the process. I have defaulted to using the weaver's knot to join threads, but you can use the reef knot if you prefer.

## Trimming Smooth Text Blocks

Traditionally, books are trimmed with a book-binding plough, but since ploughs are not accessible to the average person, here's how you can trim your text blocks at home.

Start by preparing a fresh blade or a recently snapped blade, which will make the cutting easier. Stand while cutting if you can, to gain more leverage. Working on the cutting mat, anchor a non-slip ruler on the edge of the text block, and hold firmly throughout the whole process.

Square your shoulders towards the book and pull the utility knife from head to tail along the ruler edge with medium pressure (image M). Keep the pressure even throughout, and make as many cuts as you need, letting the blade do the work.

Pressing too hard or going too fast will cause rough cuts. Make sure the blade is perpendicular to the cutting mat to avoid cutting at an angle. If you're cutting the book with the covers attached, place a cutting mat between the back cover and the text block before trimming.

Alternatively, the text block can be cut in small sections, 2 to 3 signatures at a time. This might result in some unevenness, but it could make the process more manageable. Place the cutting mat edge under the top 3 signatures and trim. Then, move the cutting mat lower and use the previous signature as a guide for the next cut.

To further smooth the edges, press the text block firmly while exposing the fore edge, and remove imperfections with fine grit sandpaper (image N).

Cutting the fore edge of a text block by hand is one of the most challenging parts of learning bookbinding. It will take practice, so keep at it!

Tip: If you're making a mixed media or watercolor sketchbook, avoid the need to trim the fore edge by tearing heavyweight paper to create soft edges.

# a guide to the projects

I've organized the projects according to the complexity of the book structure and level of difficulty (out of 3 stars).

If this is your first time bookbinding, get your feet wet by starting with the first project, Pamphlet Stitch Binding (page 30), to make softcover notebooks.

If you want to dive into making hardcover books with Case Binding (page 138), try the French Link Stitch (page 46) first, which is the foundational sewing method that is used for all of the flat-back and round-back projects.

The instructions mention terms, such as signatures, head, tail, fore edge, endpapers and more. Flip to Book Anatomy (page 8) to familiarize yourself with the different parts of a book so that you can follow along.

Set aside some time to prepare the materials listed in each project. Papers are listed with specific sizes to be cut. Having all the materials pre-cut and tools ready to use will make the process more enjoyable. Do your best to find papers with the correct grain, but if it's a challenge, don't let it stop you from trying a binding. With the exception of the first few simpler bindings, reserve at least a day to complete each book project.

Now let's make some books!

# softcover books

*approachable notebooks for every occasion*

Starting off with simple and satisfying bindings, these projects are perfect for making lightweight notebooks and journals. The covers feature card stock paper and fabric, making them easy to decorate and personalize.

## Pamphlet Stitch and Chain Stitch
### *Notebooks and Zines*

- - - - - - - - - - - - - - - - - - - - - - - - - - - - - - - - - - - - - - - - - - - -

These simple starter stitches will get you hooked on bookbinding. When I first learned about them, I made more notebooks than I can count. They're excellent for making thin, softcover journals and sketchbooks. They're also great for adding a handmade touch to self-published content like zines and chapbooks. If you have some scrap paper saved up, make notebooks with them using these quick bindings!

There are two variations of the pamphlet stitch, one with 3 holes and another with 5 holes. Instructions for the chain stitch follows. Each stitch requires the same materials.

- - - - - - - - - - - - - - - - - - - - - - - - - - - - - - - - - - - - - - - - - - - -

**Difficulty:** ★

**New skills:** folding, punching holes, sewing, trimming fore edge

- - - - - - - - - - - - - - - - - - - - - - - - - - - - - - - - - - - - - - - - - - - -

## materials

- 10 sheets of 8½ x 11 inch (21.6 x 27.9 cm) writing paper or sketch paper, 60–80lb (90–120gsm) text weight
- 1 sheet of 8½ x 11 inch (21.6 x 27.9 cm) card stock paper, 80–100lb (216–270gsm) cover weight
- Waxed linen thread, any gauge

## tools

- Bone folder
- Metal ruler
- Pencil
- Cutting mat
- Clips (optional)
- Awl
- Scissors
- Needle
- Utility knife

## Preparing the Pages and Cover

*No matter which variation you are interested in making from this project, start with these two steps first.*

I.    Start by folding all 10 sheets of writing or sketch paper in half, with the short edges meeting each other. You just created a signature, which should measure 5½ x 8½ inches (14 x 21.6 cm). Hold down the signature with your non-dominant hand to keep the corners aligned. Holding the length of the bone folder at a 45-degree angle, crease and sharpen the fold by pressing and gliding the edge of the bone folder along the folded edge of the signature. Flip it vertically and crease the fold with the bone folder one more time.

2.    Fold the card stock paper in half, the same way as the signature. Crease the fold with the bone folder. This will be the notebook cover. Place the signature in the cover and ensure the top and bottom edges of the book are flush. The outer edge (fore edge) of the pages will extend slightly beyond the cover. The book is ready to be sewn. Continue on to the desired stitch to complete the notebook.

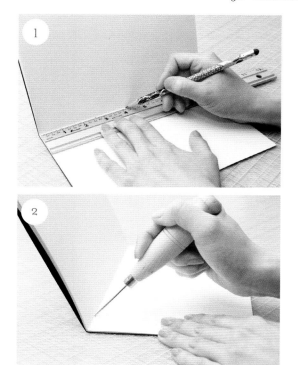

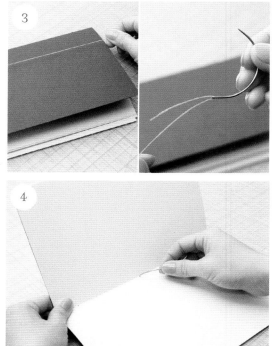

## 3-Hole Pamphlet Stitch

*The 3-hole pamphlet stitch forms two stitches on the spine. It's best for making notebooks with under 20 pages. Use the 5-hole pamphlet stitch (page 34) for notebooks with more pages.*

I.   Open the prepared pages and cover from page 31 at the middle and place your ruler up against the fold on the inside. Line up the zero with the left edge of the book. With a pencil, mark three dots on the fold at the following measurements: 1 inch (2.5 cm), 4¼ inches (10.8 cm), and 7½ inches (19 cm). The second dot marks the halfway point.

2.   Working on the cutting mat, anchor the notebook with your non-dominant hand to prevent shifting. You can use clips to keep the sheets together. Hold the awl at a 45-degree angle and punch three holes into the fold at each pencil mark. Pierce the paper until the needle tip is visible on the other side and do not enlarge the holes.

3.   Measure the waxed linen thread to two times the length of the book and cut with scissors. Thread the needle with one end and pull it through 1 to 2 inches (2.5 to 5 cm). Fold the thread and pinch flat with your fingers.

4.   For the sewing process, each hole will be referred to as sewing stations 1, 2, and 3, going from left to right with the book open towards you. Starting on the inside, sew out through station 2 (center hole) and pull until there is a tail that is about 2 inches (5 cm).

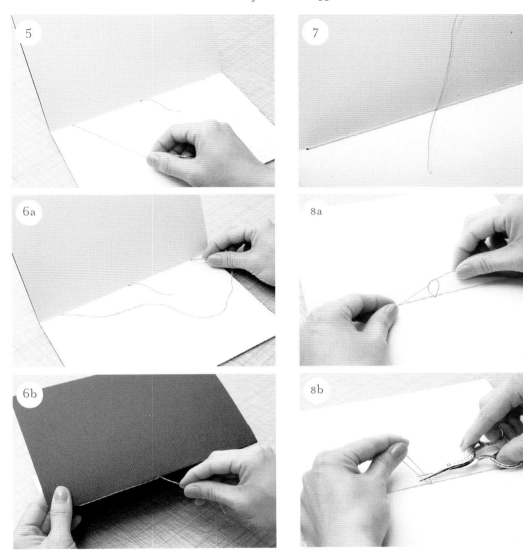

5. Sew in through station 1 to the inside, being careful not to pull the thread out of the book.

6. Sew out through station 3 and in through station 2 to meet the starting end of the thread.

7. Remove the needle and move the two thread ends to either side of the middle stitch.

8. Pull the thread ends taut, then tie an overhand knot (page 23). Cut the excess thread.

9. Trim the fore edge with the utility knife and metal ruler (instructions on page 25).

## 5-Hole Pamphlet Stitch

*The 5-hole pamphlet stitch forms four stitches on the spine instead of two. Since there are more sewing stations, this stitch is slightly stronger for notebooks with more pages.*

1. Open the prepared pages and cover from page 31 at the middle and place your ruler up against the fold on the inside. Line up the zero with the left edge of the book. With a pencil, mark five dots on the fold at the following measurements: 1 inch (2.5 cm), 2⅝ inches (6.7 cm), 4¼ inches (10.8 cm), 5⅞ inches (14.9 cm), and 7½ inches (19 cm). The third dot marks the halfway point.

2. Working on the cutting mat, anchor the notebook with your non-dominant hand to prevent shifting. You can use clips to keep the sheets together. Hold the awl at a 45-degree angle and punch five holes into the fold at each pencil mark. Pierce the paper until the needle tip is visible on the other side and do not enlarge the holes.

3. Measure the waxed linen thread to two times the length of the book and cut with scissors. Thread the needle with one end and pull it through 1 to 2 inches (2.5 to 5 cm). Fold the thread and pinch flat with your fingers.

4. For the sewing process, each hole will be referred to as sewing stations 1 to 5 going from left to right with the book open towards you. Starting on the inside, sew out through station 3 (center hole) and pull until there is a tail that is about 2 inches (5 cm).

5. Sew through station 2 to the inside, being careful to not pull the thread out of the book.

6. Sew through station 1 to the outside and back into station 2 to the inside.

7. Sew through station 4 to the outside.

**Variations:** Use alternative threads like embroidery floss, thin ribbon or jute cord. Ensure that the sewing stations and the eye of the needle are wide enough to allow for the thickness of the thread to pass through. You can also switch the sewing sequence to start on the outside rather than on the inside, and use the thread ends as decoration.

8. Sew through station 5 to the inside and back through station 4 to the outside.

9. Sew in through station 3 to meet the starting end of the thread.

10. Remove the needle and move the two thread ends to either side of the middle stitch.

11. Pull the thread ends taut, then tie an overhand knot (page 23). Cut the excess thread.

12. Trim the fore edge with the utility knife and metal ruler (instructions on page 25).

## Chain Stitch

*Chain stitch is a strong and charming stitch pattern for sewing notebooks. A chain is formed at each sewing station after the first one is created.*

1. Open the book at the middle and place your ruler up against the fold on the inside. Line up the zero with the left edge of the book. With a pencil, mark eleven dots on the fold at the following measurements: ½ inch (1.3 cm), 1¼ inches (3.2 cm), 2 inches (5 cm), 2¾ inches (7 cm), 3½ inches (8.9 cm), 4¼ inches (10.8 cm), 5 inches (12.7 cm), 5¾ inches (14.6 cm), 6½ inches (16.5 cm), 7¼ inches (18.4 cm), and 8 inches (20.3 cm). Each dot should be spaced ¾ inch (1.9 cm) apart.

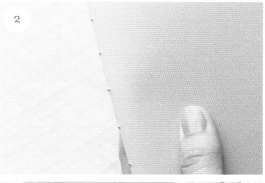

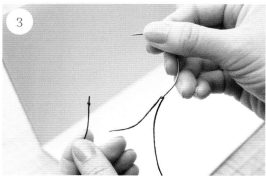

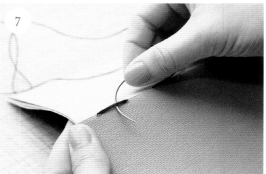

2. Working on the cutting mat, anchor the notebook with your non-dominant hand to prevent shifting. You can use clips to keep the sheets together. Hold the awl at a 45-degree angle and punch eleven holes into the fold at each pencil mark, making sure the head and tail edges remain flush. Pierce the paper until the needle tip is visible on the other side and do not enlarge the holes.

Tip: Try to not veer off the folds when punching holes. This can be more difficult with more pages, so take your time. Fold the book to guide the awl through if necessary.

3. Measure the waxed linen thread to three and a half times the length of the book and cut with scissors. Tie an overhand knot (page 23) on one end. Thread the needle with the other end and pull it through 1 to 2 inches (2.5 to 5 cm). Fold the thread and pinch flat with your fingers.

4. For the sewing process, each hole will be referred to as sewing stations 1 to 11 going from left to right with the book open towards you. Starting on the inside, sew out through station 1 and pull all the way to the knot.

5. Sew through station 2 to the inside and back through station 1 to the outside.

6. Sew through station 2 to the inside and through station 3 to the outside. There should be a double stitch between stations 1 and 2, which functions as the first chain stitch.

7. Sew up or down behind the double stitch between stations 1 and 2 on the outside spine. Pull taut and sew back through station 3 to the inside.

8a

8b

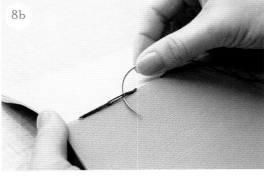

9

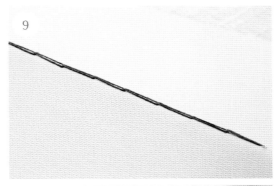

10

8. Sew through the next station to the outside and loop the needle behind the previous chain stitch on the spine. Pull taut and sew back into the station you came out of to create a new chain.

9. Repeat step 8 until you reach the last hole and your needle is on the inside.

10. Tie a half hitch knot (page 23) with your needle and cut the excess thread.

11. Trim the fore edge with the utility knife and metal ruler (instructions on page 25).

To finish the notebooks, weigh down the notebooks for a few hours to flatten. Slimmer notebooks are also achieved through folding along the paper grain (page 20). You can round the corners to prevent them from curling with use. Personalize the covers with labels, bookplates, stamps or stickers.

# Perfect Binding
## *Notepads and No-Sew Books*

- - - - - - - - - - - - - - - - - - - - - - - - - - - - - - - - - - - - - - - - - - - - -

*Perfect binding is a fun way to make a book without sewing. The book structure consists of loose-leaf papers that are held together by a glued spine. You may have seen this binding most commonly used for commercially made books, such as paperback novels, catalogues and magazines. Using pH-neutral or acid-free PVA glue is important so that the glue won't become brittle over time, and the spine remains flexible and strong. Perfect bound books typically have a gutter and don't lay flat when opened.*

*In this project, the text block you'll be making can also be used as a tear-away notepad. To complete the book, I'll show you how to make and attach a card stock cover.*

- - - - - - - - - - - - - - - - - - - - - - - - - - - - - - - - - - - - - - - - - - - - -

### Difficulty: ★

**New skills:** working with paper grain, pressing, gluing, creating a continuous soft cover, scoring

- - - - - - - - - - - - - - - - - - - - - - - - - - - - - - - - - - - - - - - - - - - - -

## materials

- 50 sheets of 4¼ x 5½ inch (10.8 x 14 cm) paper (quarter sheet of letter size paper), 60–80lb (90–120gsm) text weight, grain long
- Scrap paper for clips
- PVA glue
- Wet cloth for cleaning hands (optional)
- 1 sheet of 8½ x 11 inch (21.6 x 27.9 cm) or larger card stock paper, 80–100lb (216–270gsm) cover weight, grain long or short
- Waste sheets for gluing

## tools

- 2 bulldog or binder clips, at least 1 inch (2.5 cm) wide
- 2 large boxy weights (like heavy books)
- Tray for glue
- Small glue brush
- Utility knife
- Cutting mat
- Pencil
- Metal ruler
- Bone folder
- Scoring tool (optional)
- Weights (optional)

## Making the Text Block

Before beginning, check that the sheets of paper are the same size with flush edges. A flush spine edge is important for binding each sheet evenly. Also confirm that the grain of the paper runs lengthwise (page 20). It's important that the grain direction is parallel to the spine to prevent the papers from rippling heavily when glued and to allow the book to open smoothly.

I.   Bring the 50 sheets of paper together by tapping the long edge on the desk, making sure the sheets are flush at the bottom. This edge will be the spine.

2.   Holding the sheets together firmly, apply a clip on each short edge, about ½ inch (1.3 cm) away from the spine. Slip scrap paper under the clips if you are concerned about the clips making impressions into the pages.

3.   Prop up the clamped text block between two boxy weights with the spine facing up.

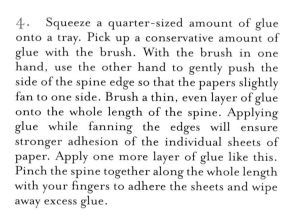

4. Squeeze a quarter-sized amount of glue onto a tray. Pick up a conservative amount of glue with the brush. With the brush in one hand, use the other hand to gently push the side of the spine edge so that the papers slightly fan to one side. Brush a thin, even layer of glue onto the whole length of the spine. Applying glue while fanning the edges will ensure stronger adhesion of the individual sheets of paper. Apply one more layer of glue like this. Pinch the spine together along the whole length with your fingers to adhere the sheets and wipe away excess glue.

Tip: Keep a wet cloth on your desk to wipe your hands clean.

5. Repeat this gluing method by fanning the papers to the other side. Brush two thin layers of glue along the whole length of the spine. Pinch the spine edge together with your fingers and wipe away excess glue.

Tip: Perfect Binding relies on the glue spine to keep the pages together and allow the book to open and close. It's important that there is enough glue for the spine to form and function, so be sure to let each coat dry to touch before applying the next coat.

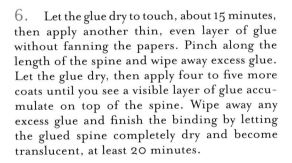

6. Let the glue dry to touch, about 15 minutes, then apply another thin, even layer of glue without fanning the papers. Pinch along the length of the spine and wipe away excess glue. Let the glue dry, then apply four to five more coats until you see a visible layer of glue accumulate on top of the spine. Wipe away any excess glue and finish the binding by letting the glued spine completely dry and become translucent, at least 20 minutes.

Tip: Rinse your glue brush or leave it in a cup of water while it's still wet to prevent glue from settling into the bristles. Dry off the brush before using it again.

7. Remove the clips from the text block and test the binding by flipping the pages. Perfect Binding doesn't allow the book to open completely, so use gentle force. The glued spine should stay intact and be slightly flexible. A cracking spine can mean that there wasn't enough fanning of the spine for the first glue coats, or too much glue was applied. If this happens, you can try to repair the crack with thin coats of glue or start over by trimming off the glued edge and re-applying the glue binding.

8. If you prefer, trim with the utility knife and metal ruler for smooth edges (instructions on page 25).

9. You can use the book as-is, or as a tear-away notepad. Continue on for instructions to make a protective soft cover for the book.

## Making the Cover

Like the text block, the cover piece should have the grain running parallel to the spine, so that scoring and folding is easier and neater. If you have an 8½ x 11–inch (21.6 x 27.9–cm) card stock sheet, identify the paper grain (page 20) to prepare for the cover construction. Long grain letter size paper will require an extra attachment to complete the cover. For this project, I'm using a 12 x 12–inch (30.5 x 30.5–cm) card stock paper.

10. Lay down the card stock paper in front of you, with the decorative side down. If the paper is long grain, position the sheet with the short edge on top. If the paper is short grain, position the long edge on top. Position square card stock sheets with the grain running up and down. Make sure the top edge is straight and square.

11. Working on the cutting mat, line up the text block on the upper left corner of the card stock paper. With a pencil, mark the text block length on the left-side edge. Line up the text block to the upper right corner and mark the text block length on the right-side edge. Remove the text block and line up the ruler along the points. Anchor the ruler and cut across the sheet with the utility knife. For long grain cover paper, save the cut piece for use in step 17.

12. On the top edge of the card stock paper, mark 1 inch (2.5 cm) from the left side. Lay down the text block with the spine on the right. Line up the left edge of the text block at the 1-inch (2.5 cm) marker and anchor it with your left hand. Using the bone folder, lift the cover paper up from the right side and make a fold by pressing the edge of the bone folder against the spine. Glide the bone folder along the whole length, with the cover paper making a 90-degree angle.

13. Continue to hold down the text block with your left hand. Use your right hand to press the cover paper flat against the spine and wrap the cover over the spine edge. Press along the whole length of the edge to make another fold.

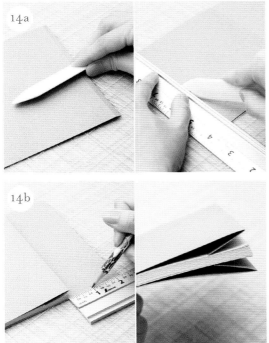

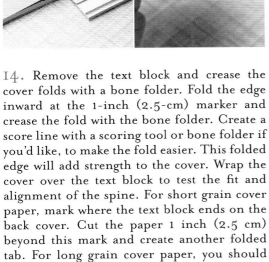

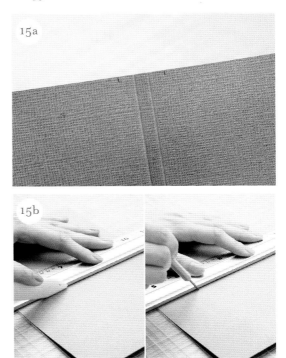

14. Remove the text block and crease the cover folds with a bone folder. Fold the edge inward at the 1-inch (2.5-cm) marker and crease the fold with the bone folder. Create a score line with a scoring tool or bone folder if you'd like, to make the fold easier. This folded edge will add strength to the cover. Wrap the cover over the text block to test the fit and alignment of the spine. For short grain cover paper, mark where the text block ends on the back cover. Cut the paper 1 inch (2.5 cm) beyond this mark and create another folded tab. For long grain cover paper, you should have one side (the back cover) that is short.

15. Place the cover piece face-down on the cutting mat. Mark two points on the top edge, ¼ inch (6 mm) from either side of the spine folds, one on the front cover and one on the back cover. Line up the ruler edge at the first point, parallel to the spine, and make a score line by pressing and gliding the tip of the bone folder or scoring tool onto the cover paper with medium pressure. Create a score line at the second point as well. These will be the cover hinges. Erase the pencil marks. For short grain cover paper, the cover is complete. Skip to step 19 (page 45) for installing the cover. For long grain cover paper, continue on to attach the remaining piece.

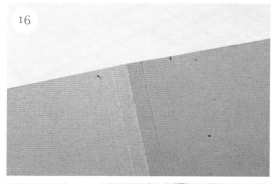

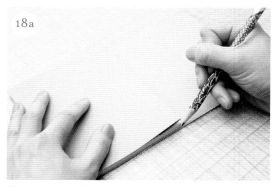

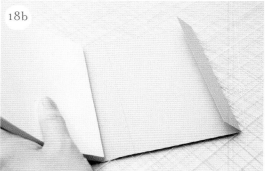

17. Pick up the card stock piece that was cut off in step 2. Measure and cut it to the same length as the cover paper. With a waste sheet, mask the longer cover piece at the score line, exposing the ½-inch (1.3-cm) tab. Brush a thin layer of PVA glue onto the exposed tab, being careful to not brush glue onto the score line. Attach the cover piece onto the tab with the score line visible. Rub the sheets together with the bone folder and let dry.

16. On the short side of the cover paper (the back cover), measure and mark ½ inch (1.3 cm) from the score line on the top edge. Make a vertical cut at that mark to create a tab.

18. Wrap the cover over the text block and mark where the text block ends on the back cover. Cut the paper 1 inch (2.5 cm) beyond this mark and create another folded tab.

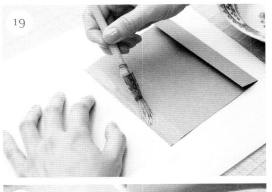

## Installing the Cover

19. Open the cover flat on a waste sheet. Brush a thin layer of glue onto the inner spine of the cover within the score lines. Avoid over-gluing to prevent glue from oozing out when the cover is installed.

20. Carefully place the text block spine onto the cover piece, checking for alignment on all four edges, then lift one cover and press along the glued strip with the bone folder. Lift and attach the remaining side.

21. Press all three sides of the spine with your fingers, pushing the cover towards the fore edge. Smooth out any bumps with the bone folder. Set aside to let dry completely, at least 1 hour, before opening the book. Optionally, you can place weights on top of the book to ensure the book dries flat.

22. Attach the 1-inch (2.5-cm) tabs on the inner covers by using a tiny drop of glue on each corner. Press to adhere.

# French Link Stitch
## *Minimal Lay-Flat Notebook*

- - - - - - - - - - - - - - - - - - - - - - - - - - - - - - - - - - - - - - - - - - - - - - - - - - -

*French Link Stitch is a sewing method that is considered strong enough for small- to medium-sized text blocks without the need for extra support. It's also a pretty and elegant stitch, so bookbinders will often use French links for exposed spine books. With the addition of a glue binding on the spine, this project is an excellent choice for making a portable, softcover notebook with a higher page count.*

*You can easily modify the number of pages for this project. I recommend a spine thickness of no more than ¾ inch (1.9 cm) after it's sewn to minimize spine swell (see page 181 to learn more).*

- - - - - - - - - - - - - - - - - - - - - - - - - - - - - - - - - - - - - - - - - - - - - - - - - - -

### Difficulty: ★ ★

**New skills:** multi-signature sewing, pressing and gluing the spine,
French link and kettle stitches, trimming a text block, making a lay-flat book

- - - - - - - - - - - - - - - - - - - - - - - - - - - - - - - - - - - - - - - - - - - - - - - - - - -

## materials

- 35 sheets of 8½ x 11 inch (21.6 x 27.9 cm) writing or sketch paper, 60–80lb (90–120gsm) text weight, grain short
- 2 sheets of 8½ x 11 inch (21.6 x 27.9 cm) card stock paper, 80–100lb (216–270gsm) cover weight, grain short (preferred) or long
- Strip of stiff paper cut to 8½ inches (21.6 cm) in length and 2–3 inches (5–7.6 cm) in width
- Waxed linen thread, ²⁵/₃ gauge (thin)
- 2 pieces of scrap book board larger than 5½ x 8½ inches (14 x 21.6 cm) with long side clear taped
- PVA glue
- Waste sheets for gluing

## tools

- Bone folder
- Ruler
- Pencil
- Cutting mat
- Awl
- Scissors
- Needle
- Pressing equipment: book press, clamps or weights
- Glue brush
- Utility knife
- Fine grit sandpaper (optional)
- Corner rounder (optional)

## Preparing the Signatures

I.  Start by folding five sheets of the writing paper in half, with the short edges meeting each other. Crease the fold with the bone folder. Flip the folded papers vertically and crease the fold one more time. This is the first signature, which should measure 5½ x 8½ inches (14 x 21.6 cm). Make six more signatures like this with the remaining sheets.

2.  Fold each sheet of card stock paper in half and crease the fold with the bone folder. Place each card stock folio on the top and bottom of the signature stack. These will be the front and back covers, which will be sewn along with the text block.

3

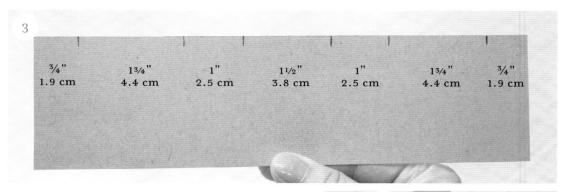

| ¾"<br>1.9 cm | 1¾"<br>4.4 cm | 1"<br>2.5 cm | 1½"<br>3.8 cm | 1"<br>2.5 cm | 1¾"<br>4.4 cm | ¾"<br>1.9 cm |
|---|---|---|---|---|---|---|

3. The strip of stiff paper, which is the same length as the signatures, will be the guide for punching holes. With a ruler and pencil, measure and mark ¾ inch (1.9 cm) on the long edge on the stiff paper from the left- and right-side edges. Line up the zero of the ruler with the left-side edge, then mark four more points at the following measurements: 2½ inches (6.4 cm), 3½ inches (8.9 cm), 5 inches (12.7 cm), and 6 inches (15.2 cm). There should be six marks in total. French links, measuring 1 inch (2.5 cm), will be sewn between the 2nd and 3rd marks and the 4th and 5th marks. The image shows the spacing between the marks.

4. Working on the cutting mat, place the punching guide up against the fold of the first signature, making sure the head and tail edges are flush. Hold the awl at a 45-degree angle and punch holes through the fold at each point marked on the guide. Pierce the paper until the needle tip is visible on the other side, but don't push the needle further to avoid enlarging the holes. Repeat this step for the remaining eight signatures. Hold all the signatures together and make sure the holes are aligned at the spine. Hole alignment is important for achieving flush head and tail edges of the book after the text block is sewn.

4a

4b
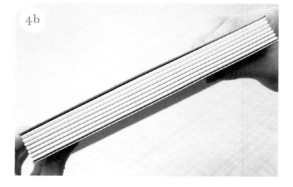

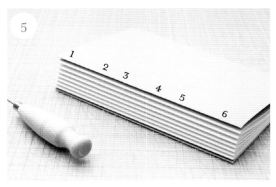

## Sewing - French Link Stitch

The book will be sewn from cover to cover, and bottom to top. In this project, the covers count as signatures. Each hole in the signatures will be referred to as a sewing station and numbered 1–6 going from left to right with the spine facing you. Using a thin thread is important for minimizing spine swell (page 181).

5.  Measure thread out to be the length of the spine multiplied by the number of signatures, then cut the thread with scissors. Thread one end with the needle.

Note: You can start sewing with a shorter length of thread, which is more manageable and is less likely to tangle. Add more thread during the sewing process by tying the weaver's knot on the inside of the signatures, as demonstrated on page 24.

6.  Position the signatures with the spine facing you. Pick up all but the last signature and flip them over in front of you. This is important because it is easy to mix up the alignment of the holes if the signatures are placed randomly. Starting from the outside of the signature, sew in through the 6th (right-most) station and pull the thread until there is a 2-inch (5-cm) tail.

7.  Sew out through station 5, being careful not to pull the thread out of the signature. Then sew in through station 4, out through station 3, in through station 2, and out through station 1. Hold the starting and working ends of the thread and pull taut.

8

9b

9a

10

8. Pick up a new signature and flip it onto the working book. At a glance, match the alignment of the sewing stations. Sew in through station 1 of the new signature to the inside. Hold the signatures together with your non-dominant hand to prevent shifting.

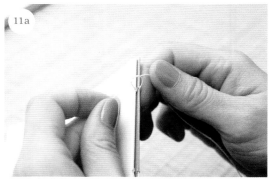

11a

9. It's time to sew the first French link! Sew out through station 2 to the spine. Sew up behind the stitch on the previous signature, then sew through station 3 to the inside.

10. Sew out through station 4 to the spine. Create another French link by sewing up behind the stitch on the previous signature, then sew through station 5 to the inside.

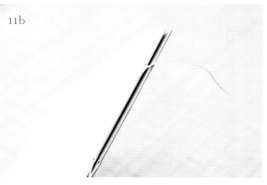

11b

11. Sew out through station 6 to meet the starting end of the thread. Pull the working thread taut towards the right, then tie an overhand knot with both ends to lock the first 2 signatures together.

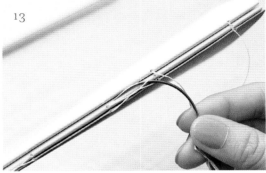

## Odd-Numbered Signature

12. Pick up a new signature and flip it onto the working book. At a glance, match the alignment of the sewing stations. Sew in through station 6 of the new signature.

13. Sew out through station 5 to the spine. Create a French link by sewing up behind the stitch on the previous signature, then sew through station 4 to the inside.

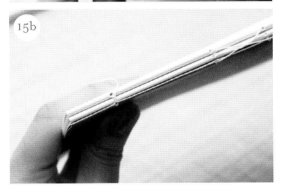

14. Sew out through station 3 to the spine. Create a French link by sewing up behind the stitch on the previous signature, then sew through station 2 to the inside.

15. Sew out through station 1 and pull the thread taut towards the left. Create a kettle stitch (page 23) with the stitch directly below. Kettle stitches are intended to lock signatures together.

Tip: When increasing thread tension, pull towards the direction of sewing, parallel to the spine, to prevent accidental ripping at the holes.

## Even-Numbered Signature

16. Pick up a new signature and flip it onto the working book. At a glance, match the alignment of the sewing stations. Sew in through station 1 of the new signature.

17. Sew out through station 2 to the spine. Create a French link by sewing up behind the stitch on the previous signature, then sew through station 3 to the inside.

18. Sew out through station 4 to the spine. Create a French link by sewing up behind the stitch on the previous signature, then sew through station 5 to the inside.

19. Sew out through station 6 and pull the thread taut towards the right. Create a kettle stitch (page 23) with the stitch directly below.

20. For the subsequent signatures, repeat steps 12 through 15 for odd-numbered signatures, and repeat steps 16 through 19 for even-numbered signatures. You should see the French links resemble a zig-zag pattern on the spine.

21. When you have sewn on the last signature and finished with a kettle stitch, cut the working thread to about 1 inch (2.5 cm). It's normal that the signatures are loose. The binding will be more stable after the spine is glued.

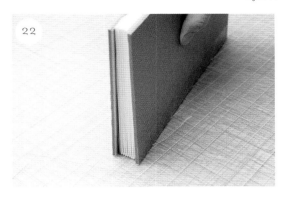

## Pressing and Gluing the Spine

The French links and glue work together to add structure and flexibility to the spine. Prepare the glue brush by dry brushing your fingers to remove any dust or loose bristles. Since the glued spine will be exposed in this project, it's important that the glue dries clear of dust.

When pressing the spine, aim to reduce the thickness of the spine (spine swell) slightly to be level with the fore edge as much as possible. It's important to not over-tighten which can cause the signatures to collapse or fall out of alignment along the spine.

22. Place the text block in between two scrap book boards, with their taped edges lined up with the spine. The taped edges will prevent the text block from sticking to the boards. Tap the text block and board sandwich on the desk to bring the signatures to alignment along the spine.

> Note: When pressing the text block, aim to align the signatures at the head and tail as best as possible for smooth and level edges.

23. Gluing the spine is easiest if the text block is pressed and propped up vertically with the spine facing up. Apply consistent medium pressing force on the signature folds along the spine. Here are a few ways you can press the spine.

• If you have a book press, slide the sandwiched text block into the press with ¼ inch (6 mm) of the spine edge extending beyond the edge of the press. Press the text block and lift the press to stand vertically.

• Using C-clamps or spring clamps, press the sandwiched text block, making sure there is even pressure along the spine. Avoid pinching any part of the spine and over-tightening the clamps. Prop up the text block between two boxy weights to stand (image 23).

• The text block can be pressed under weights as it lays horizontally. Place the sandwiched text block in between two boxy weights, such as heavy books. Have ¼ inch (6 mm) of the spine edge extend beyond the weights so that you can work on the spine. Use stable weights to prevent shifting.

> Tip: Bookbinders use an advanced tool called a finishing press to clamp the book as it stands upright on the fore edge. The finishing press is specifically designed for spine work.

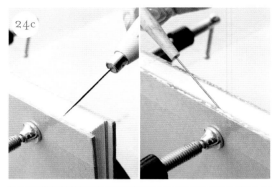

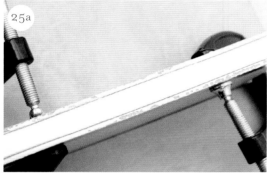

24. Cut the thread ends down to about ¼ inch (6 mm). Brush a generous layer of PVA glue along the length of the spine, but not so much that it pools and seeps in between the signatures. Using an awl or the tip of the brush handle, tuck the thread ends in between the signatures. Use the tip of the brush to stipple on glue over the links, or use your fingers to push glue into hard-to-reach areas. Cover all the gaps in the spine and let the glue dry to touch.

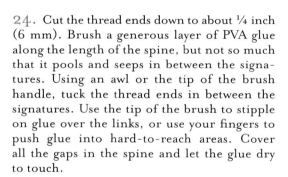

Tip: Run the tip of the awl between the outer signatures and the pressing boards to remove glue for easier detaching later.

25. Brush two to three more thin coats of glue, letting each coat dry before applying a new one. Let the glue dry completely in the press, at least 20 minutes.

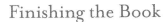

## Finishing the Book

Once the glue is dry, the book is complete. Take the book out of the press, slowly detach the pressing boards from the text block, and remove any excess dried glue. Here are some additional steps to finish and personalize the book.

26. Trim the fore edge with the utility knife and metal ruler (instructions on page 25). Since the fore edge is quite thick, use a fresh blade and hold the blade perpendicular to the cutting mat to cut a square edge, rather than a sloped edge. Clamp the book and sand the edge with fine grit sandpaper to smooth out any rough spots.

27. Round the corners to prevent them from curling with use. You can use an industrial corner rounder to round the pages all at once, or a handheld rounder, punching a few sheets at a time. Both methods work well.

28. Brush a light amount of glue on the edges of the cover folios to close them up. Avoid applying glue onto the full page, which can cause wrinkling or warping. The cover folios can also be left open and used creatively. Use the space to display stickers or add pockets. You can make your own pockets by following the instructions on page 178.

29. Decorate the cover with stamps or a simple collage.

30. Wrap the spine with bookbinding tape for extra support.

## Long Stitch with Wrap-Around Cover
### *Travel Diary*

- - - - - - - - - - - - - - - - - - - - - - - - - - - - - - - - - - - - - - - - - - - - -

*This project sparks nostalgia because it reminds me of the diaries I used to collect as a kid. The wrap-around cover makes this book an excellent keeper of secrets. The design is elevated with a quality fabric cover and a beautiful stitching pattern. Long stitch is a versatile and straightforward binding, allowing the book design to be very customizable.*

*In this project, I use wool fabric stiffened with HeatnBond®, a fusible interfacing. An alternative option is 2-mm-thick felt which is non-woven and doesn't require edge treatment. If you have sewing skills, I encourage you to sew your own double-sided cover, or even a quilted one!*

- - - - - - - - - - - - - - - - - - - - - - - - - - - - - - - - - - - - - - - - - - - - -

### Difficulty: ★ ★

**New skills:** creating a continuous fabric cover, non-adhesive
multi-signature sewing, gathering stitch, installing a ribbon closure

- - - - - - - - - - - - - - - - - - - - - - - - - - - - - - - - - - - - - - - - - - - - -

## materials

- 49 sheets of 8½ x 11–inch (21.6 x 27.9–cm) writing or sketch paper, 60–80lb (90-120gsm) text weight, grain short (preferred) or long
- 2 sheets of 10 x 19–inch (25.4 x 48.3–cm) heavyweight fabric around ¹/₁₆ inch (2 mm) when stacked
- 1 sheet of 9½ x 18½–inch (24.1 x 47–cm) HeatnBond Lite or Ultrahold or alternative double-sided fusible interfacing
- Choice of cover edge treatment (embroidery floss [for non-woven fabric], double-fold bias tape, or liquid seam sealant)
- 1-inch (2.5-cm) wide artist tape or painter's tape
- Strip of stiff paper cut to 8½ inches (21.6 cm) in length and 2–3 inches (5–7.6 cm) in width
- Waxed linen thread, any gauge
- Choice of book closure: snap button, Velcro® fastener, ribbon

## tools

- Bone folder
- Ironing board
- Flat iron
- Rotary cutter
- Ruler
- Scissors
- Non-smudge ink pen
- Cutting mat
- Awl
- Needle
- Stitch holder (or another needle)
- Fabric marker (optional)
- Tweezers or small needle-nose pliers
- Utility knife

## Folding Signatures

Using short grain paper for the pages is preferred for making flatter folds, but long grain paper will work just fine and have no effect on the function of the book.

1. Start by folding seven sheets of the writing or sketch paper in half, with the short edges meeting each other. Crease the fold with the bone folder. Flip the folded papers vertically and crease the fold one more time. This is the first signature, which should measure 5½ x 8½ inches (14 x 21.6 cm). Make six more signatures like this and set aside.

## Preparing the Cover

The cover is made by attaching two sheets of heavyweight fabric with HeatnBond fusible interfacing, which functions as an adhesive and stiffener. The final cover of this book measures 2 mm thick. If you're using a stiff, non-woven fabric, such as felt, as a stand-alone cover, skip to step 4.

2. Set up the ironing board and flat iron. Iron both pieces of fabric flat and set one aside. Place the sheet of HeatnBond, paper side up, centered on the wrong side of the fabric. Iron on the HeatnBond according to package instructions. Let the fabric cool.

5. There are several options for finishing the edges. If you're using a non-woven fabric, you can hand sew a decorative edge stitch with embroidery floss, such as the blanket stitch. Woven fabrics require edge treatment to prevent fraying. If you have a sewing machine, you can sew on double-fold bias tape. For a no-sew solution, use a liquid seam sealant, such as Dritz Fray Check®. Apply a small amount on all the edges to absorb into the fabric. Let dry for 15 to 30 minutes.

6. Wrap the cover around the signatures for a test fit. The front cover should wrap over the width of the signatures, and the back cover should overlap the front cover by about 5 inches (12.7 cm).

## Making a Sewing Guide and Punching Holes

This sewing guide will be taped onto the cover for sewing and will come in handy for punching holes into the signatures. Use a pen that doesn't smudge to prevent ink from smearing onto the book.

3. Peel off the HeatnBond paper backing and place the other piece of heavyweight fabric on top, right side up, making sure the edges line up. Iron on the top piece of fabric. If necessary, use the steam function to penetrate the thick fabric to ensure the HeatnBond's adhesion is activated throughout. Let the fabric cool.

4. Using the rotary cutter and ruler, trim all 4 edges so that the piece measures 9 x 18 inches (22.9 x 45.7 cm) and the edges are straight and square. Make sure all of the edges are attached securely with HeatnBond. If you prefer, cut round corners with scissors.

7. Cut a 10-inch (25.4-cm) piece of artist tape and place it vertically on a smooth clean surface. First, we will mark horizontal lines on the tape by starting with dots on the sides. With the pen, mark the following eight points along the length of the tape from the top: ½ inch (1.3 cm), 1¼ inches (3.2 cm), 1½ inches (3.8 cm), 4¾ inches (12.1 cm), 5¼ inches (13.3 cm), 8½ inches (21.6 cm), 8¾ inches (22.2 cm), 9½ inches (24.1 cm). Mark the same points on the other side of the tape and draw lines across the width of the tape by connecting the dots. There should be eight horizontal lines. The image shows the spacing between the marks.

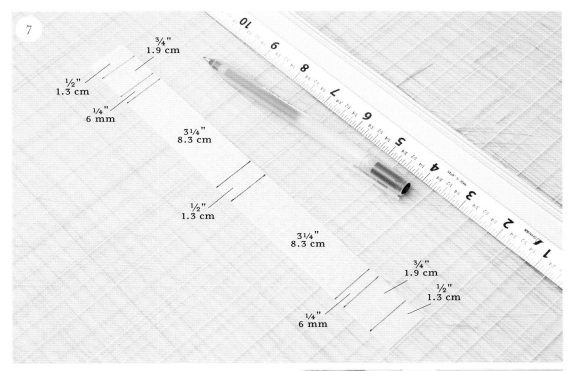

8. Now we're going to draw vertical lines to mark where each signature will be sewn. On the top and bottom edges of the tape, mark seven points spaced ⅛ inch (3 mm) apart. Connect the points by drawing lines along the length of the tape. You may need to wipe the ruler clean from residual ink. These seven vertical lines will coordinate with the seven signatures. Each intersection of the grid will be a sewing station. There should be six sewing stations per signature.

9. To apply the spine tape onto the outside cover, lay the cover flat facing down, and place one signature up to the right-side edge. Place the spine guide onto the left of the signature, matching the first and last horizontal line with the head and tail edges of the cover. Press along the tape to adhere. Remove the signature and wrap the top and bottom edges of the tape around the fabric so the tips of the tape are visible on the inside cover.

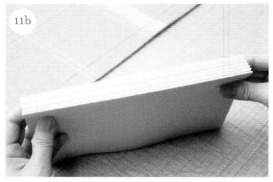

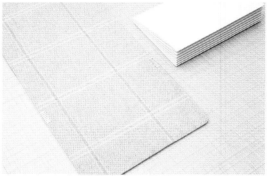

10. The strip of stiff paper, which is the same length as the signatures, will be the guide for punching holes. To make the punching guide, line up the stiff paper strip along the length of the spine tape and center it between the head and tail. With the pen, mark points on the long edge of the stiff paper at the short lines.

11. Working on the cutting mat, place the punching guide up against the fold of the first signature, making sure the head and tail edges are flush. Hold the awl at a 45-degree angle and punch holes through the fold at each point marked on the guide. Pierce the paper until the needle tip is visible on the other side and do not enlarge the holes. Repeat this step for all seven signatures. Hold all the signatures together and check that the holes are aligned.

## Sewing - Long Stitch Binding with Gathering Stitch

To set up, lay the cover open on the desk with the front cover at the bottom pointing towards you. Place the stack of signatures within arm's reach, with the spines facing towards you. We are going to sew on one signature at a time, from front cover to back cover. The holes will be numbered as sewing stations 1 to 6, going from left to right.

12. Measure and cut thread that is eight times the length of the spine. Tie a double overhand knot on one end (page 23). Thread the other end through a needle and pull it through about 1 to 2 inches (2.5 to 5 cm). Fold the thread and press it flat with your fingers.

13. Pick up the first signature. Starting from the inside of the signature, sew out through the 6th (rightmost) station and pull the thread all the way to the knot.

14a

14b

15a
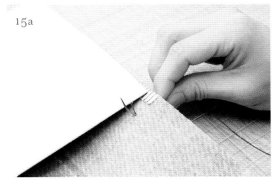

15b
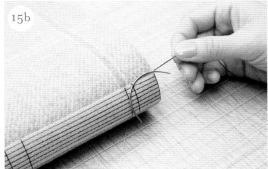

I4. Align the folded edge of the signature with the first tape lines at the head and tail. Using the signature as a guide, find the first sewing station by poking the needle through the fabric to the first intersection on the tape. You may have to try a few times. Sew through to the outside spine, pulling the signature and cover to touch.

Tip: The sewing process may feel awkward and floppy since the fabric doesn't offer much structure. Try to not sew too tightly as you'll be able to adjust the tension later on. When all the signatures are sewn on, the completed book will feel sturdy.

15c
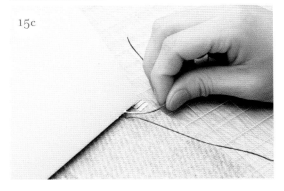

I5. Hold the signature and cover together with your non-dominant hand to prevent shifting. Sew back into the same hole of the cover but not through the signature. Pull the thread until there is a small loop on the outside spine. Be careful to not pull the thread out of the book. Hold the loop in place with a stitch holder, such as another needle. Sew through station 6 of the signature to the inside.

16a
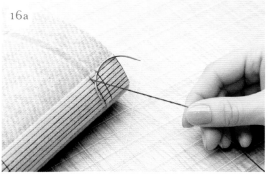

16b
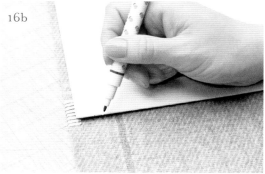

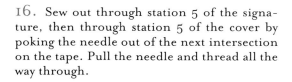

17

20
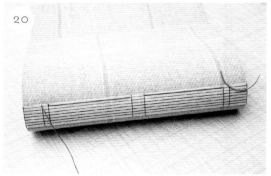

16. Sew out through station 5 of the signature, then through station 5 of the cover by poking the needle out of the next intersection on the tape. Pull the needle and thread all the way through.

Tip: To find the cover sewing stations, line up the edge of the signature with the tape markers at the head and tail. Place the needle on the fabric at the signature hole. Push through and check the outside spine to see if you have pierced through an intersection on the tape. Alternatively, if you have a fabric pen with disappearing ink, place the signature or the punching guide lined up with the markers at the head and tail, and draw dots on the fabric to mark the sewing stations. Confirm that they line up with the points on the tape by poking your needle through.

17. Sew in through station 4 of the cover, then through station 4 of the signature to the inside.

18. Sew out through station 3 of the signature, then through station 3 of the cover to the outside.

19. Sew in through station 2 of the cover, then through station 2 of the signature to the inside.

20. Sew out through station 1 of the signature, then through station 1 of the cover to the outside.

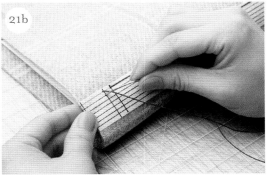

21. Let's add the next signature. With the front cover positioned towards you, pick up a new signature and place it in front of the previous one, checking that the holes are aligned between the signatures. On the outside spine, sew through station 1 of the next line on the spine tape, then sew in through station 1 of the new signature to the inside. Pull the thread and bring the signature and cover to touch.

Note: Each time a new signature is added, the position of the cover is reset to confirm alignment of the sewing stations. While sewing on a signature, you can maneuver your work however you need.

22. Sew out through station 2 of the signature, then through station 2 of the cover to the outside.

23. Sew in through station 3 of the cover, then through station 3 of the signature to the inside.

24. Sew out through station 4 of the signature, then through station 4 of the cover to the outside.

25. Sew in through station 5 of the cover, then through station 5 of the signature to the inside.

26. Sew out through station 6 of the signature, then through station 6 of the cover to the outside.

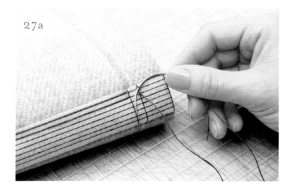

27a

27b

27. Carefully remove the stitch holder from the first signature and sew through the loop. Pull the working thread taut.

27c

Tip: You can increase thread tension by pulling the long stitches on the spine with the needle. Start with the first long stitch of the first signature, then pull on the subsequent stitches by following your sewing path until you reach your working thread. Pull until there is no more slack, but do not over-tighten. I suggest doing this after sewing on every two signatures.

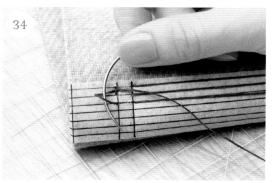

34

28. With the front cover positioned towards you, pick up a new signature and place it in front of the previous one, checking that the holes are aligned between the signatures. On the outside spine, sew through station 6 of the next line on the spine tape, then through station 6 of the new signature to the inside. Pull the thread and bring the signature and cover to touch.

29. Sew out through station 5 of the signature, then through station 5 of the cover to the outside.

30. Sew in through station 4 of the cover, then through station 4 of the signature to the inside.

31. Sew out through station 3 of the signature, then through station 3 of the cover to the outside.

32. Sew in through station 2 of the cover, then through station 2 of the signature to the inside.

33. Sew out through station 1 of the signature, then through station 1 of the cover to the outside.

34. Create a kettle stitch (page 23) by sewing behind the stitch between the previous signatures, then pull the thread taut.

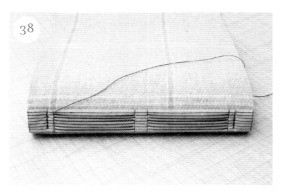

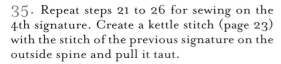

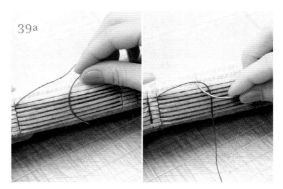

35. Repeat steps 21 to 26 for sewing on the 4th signature. Create a kettle stitch (page 23) with the stitch of the previous signature on the outside spine and pull it taut.

36. Repeat steps 28 to 33 for sewing on the 5th signature. Create a kettle stitch (page 23) with the stitch of the previous signature on the outside spine and pull it taut.

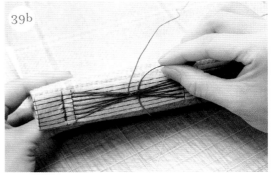

37. Repeat steps 21 to 26 for sewing on the 6th signature. Create a kettle stitch (page 23) with the stitch of the previous signature on the outside spine and pull it taut.

38. Attach the 7th and final signature at station 6 by sewing in through the cover and signature. Sew out through station 5 of the signature, then through station 5 of the cover to the outside. Close the book and spin the book around so that the spine is facing you, and the 7th signature is on top. Let's begin the gathering stitch.

For the remaining steps, the sewing stations will be renumbered as 1 to 6, going from left to right on the spine side.

39. The gathering stitch is a decorative stitch that creates a bow shape. Bring the needle down behind all of the long stitches. Sew up through the loop of the working thread and pull it taut. Bring the needle down behind the stitches again and sew up through the loop of the working thread to secure the gathering stitch.

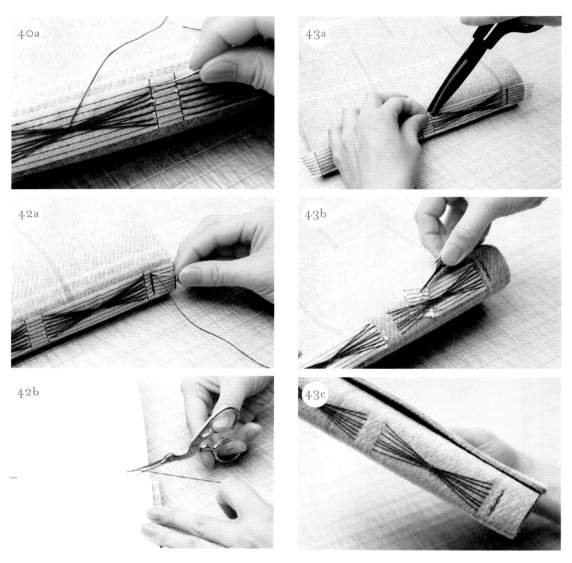

40. Sew in through station 3 of the cover and signature, then out through station 4 of the signature and cover back to the spine.

41. Repeat step 39 to create another gathering stitch. Sew in through station 5 of the cover and signature, then out through station 6 of the signature and cover. Create a kettle stitch by sewing behind the stitch of the previous signature and pull it taut.

42. Sew back in through station 6 of the cover and signature. On the inside, secure the sewing by tying a double half hitch knot (page 23). Cut the excess thread.

43. Using scissors and tweezers or pliers, carefully remove the tape from the cover without disturbing the stitching. Cut the tape along the short lines of the spine tape, being careful not to cut the thread. Peel the tape away from the sewing stations to remove.

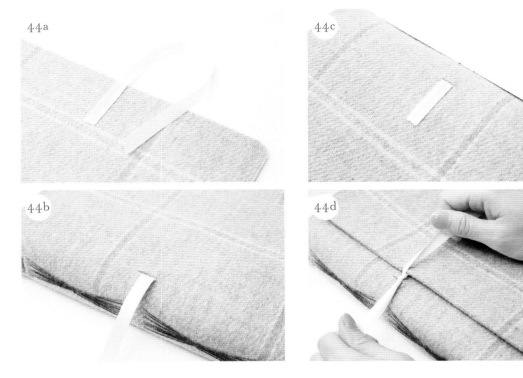

44a

44b

44c

44d

44. To add a closure to the book, you can sew on snap buttons, Velcro fasteners or ribbon. I chose to attach ribbon ties with fabric glue. Glue on a piece of ribbon on the edge of the inner back cover. On the front cover, cut a slit near the spine where the cover overlaps and treat it with liquid seam sealant. Then thread the ribbon through and glue one end to the inner cover. Seal the edges of the ribbon with a lighter. The ribbon is ready to be tied after the glue is dry.

**Sewn variation:** If you have sewing experience, you may choose to create your own double-sided cover. Stiffen the fabric to your liking, sew the fabrics around the edges' right sides together and then turn it right side out. Press with an iron for clean, finished edges. The final cover should measure 9 x 18 inches (22.9 x 45.7 cm).

# hardcover books with exposed sewing

*creative bindings with flair*

Books that feature exposed sewn spines are intriguing and offer interesting design opportunities. These structures can inspire creative purposes, such as writing, drawing, painting and scrapbooking. Have fun choosing thread colors and learning new sewing methods!

# Japanese Stab Binding
## *Notebook with Loose-Leaf Paper*

- - - - - - - - - - - - - - - - - - - - - - - - - - - - - - - - - - - - - - - -

*Stab binding was widely used during the Edo Period (1603-1867) in Japan for commercially-made books, which were printed with woodblocks. Used for binding books across Asia, stab-bound books often featured soft cover material, a narrow title strip and thin pages made of locally available materials, such as hemp and mulberry. Book structures and designs varied across different cultures.*

*Stab binding makes a lovely choice for binding poetry, short stories and other printed material. It's also an elegant way to make a notebook with light-weight paper for writing and calligraphy. While traditional stab-bound books are made with soft covers, this project introduces making a hard cover with a hinge.*

- - - - - - - - - - - - - - - - - - - - - - - - - - - - - - - - - - - - - - - -

### Difficulty: ★ ★

**New skills:** making a hard cover with hinge, working with book cloth, turning in cover material, attaching endpapers

- - - - - - - - - - - - - - - - - - - - - - - - - - - - - - - - - - - - - - - -

## materials

- 2 sheets of 5¾ x 8⅝ inch (14.6 x 21.9 cm) book board, 0.08 inch (2 mm) thick, grain short
- 2 sheets of 7¾ x 11¼ inch (19.7 x 28.6 cm) book cloth
- Waste sheets for gluing
- PVA glue
- 1 sheet of 8½ x 11 inch (21.6 x 27.9 cm) card stock paper, 80–100lb (216–270gsm) cover weight, grain long
- 30 sheets of 5½ x 8½–inch (14 x 21.6–cm) writing or sketch paper (half sheet of letter size paper), 60–80lb (90–120gsm), grain short
- Clean scrap paper for clips
- Foam or corrugated cardboard (optional)
- Waxed linen thread, thin preferred

## tools

- Cutting mat
- Ruler
- Pencil
- Utility knife
- Glue brush
- Bone folder
- ¾-inch (1.9-cm) spacer
- Rotary cutter
- Scissors
- Heavy duty awl, hand drill or Japanese screw punch
- 2 heavy duty bulldog or binder clips, at least 1 inch (2.5 cm) wide
- Straight bookbinding needle, #18 gauge (suggested)
- Rubber or silicone thimbles (optional)

## Making the Covers

I.   Let's create the front cover board with a space for the hinge. On the cutting mat, place a sheet of book board with the long edge on top. On the top edge, use your ruler and pencil to measure and mark two points from the left side: one at ¾ inch (1.9 cm) and the second at 1⅛ inch (2.9 cm). The ⅜-inch (1-cm) space between the marks is the hinge gap. Mark the same points on the bottom edge and draw vertical lines to connect the points. Cut along these lines with the utility knife and ruler. Keep the three pieces of board side by side.

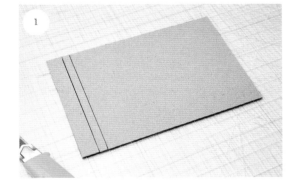

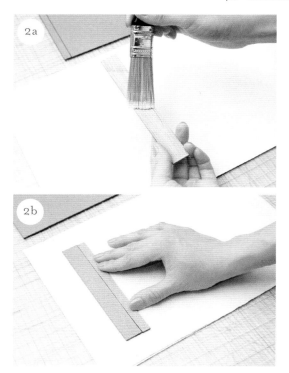

2. Place one sheet of book cloth with the paper side facing up, long edge on top, and trim a straight edge on the left side. Mark 1½ inches (3.8 cm) from the left edge and draw a vertical line with a pencil. Lay out a waste sheet on your workspace. With the glue brush, spread a thin layer of PVA glue onto the first ¾-inch (1.9-cm) piece of book board. Place it against the pencil line, centered between the head and tail.

Place the ⅜-inch (1-cm) piece of book board without any glue to the right of the piece you just laid down. Brush a thin layer of glue onto the largest piece of front cover board and place it to the right of the two smaller pieces, checking for alignment at the head and tail.

Press down on the boards gently, then remove the ⅜-inch (1-cm) piece of board for the hinge.

3. Flip the cover over so that the cloth side is facing up. Rub on the book cloth using the length of the bone folder with medium pressure. Smooth outward from the center of the board. Score the hinge by digging the tip of the bone folder into the hinge gap, pressing along the edges of the boards. This will help form a groove at the hinge, and allow for more movement when opening the cover.

Note: I made this book cloth myself using cotton linen fabric, HeatnBond and washi. Book cloth should be stiffened with a moisture barrier and backed with paper so that it will adhere to book board when glued.

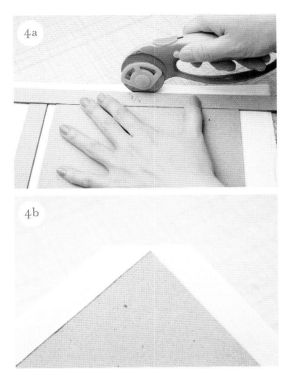

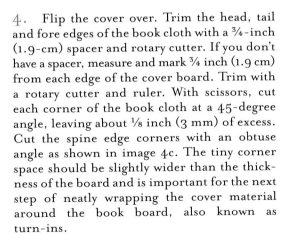

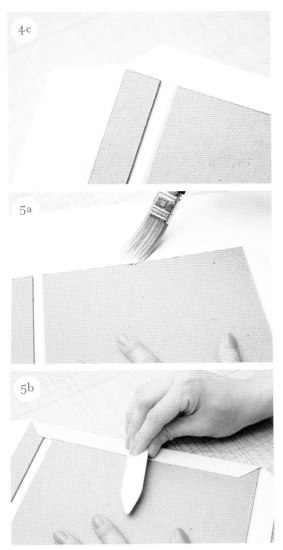

4. Flip the cover over. Trim the head, tail and fore edges of the book cloth with a ¾-inch (1.9-cm) spacer and rotary cutter. If you don't have a spacer, measure and mark ¾ inch (1.9 cm) from each edge of the cover board. Trim with a rotary cutter and ruler. With scissors, cut each corner of the book cloth at a 45-degree angle, leaving about ⅛ inch (3 mm) of excess. Cut the spine edge corners with an obtuse angle as shown in image 4c. The tiny corner space should be slightly wider than the thickness of the board and is important for the next step of neatly wrapping the cover material around the book board, also known as turn-ins.

5. Starting at the top edge of the cover, brush a thin layer of glue onto the tab of book cloth. Wrap the tab around the board and press firmly throughout. Press and smooth out the glued tab with a bone folder. Repeat for the tab on the opposite side of this cover. Press the book cloth into the hinge gap with the bone folder.

6a

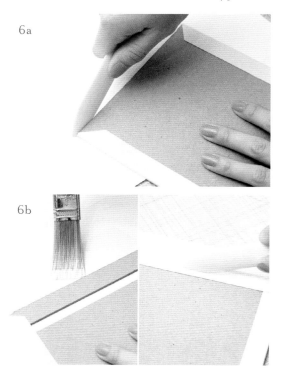

6b

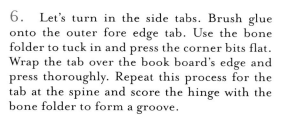

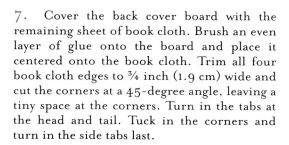

7

8

6. Let's turn in the side tabs. Brush glue onto the outer fore edge tab. Use the bone folder to tuck in and press the corner bits flat. Wrap the tab over the book board's edge and press thoroughly. Repeat this process for the tab at the spine and score the hinge with the bone folder to form a groove.

7. Cover the back cover board with the remaining sheet of book cloth. Brush an even layer of glue onto the board and place it centered onto the book cloth. Trim all four book cloth edges to ¾ inch (1.9 cm) wide and cut the corners at a 45-degree angle, leaving a tiny space at the corners. Turn in the tabs at the head and tail. Tuck in the corners and turn in the side tabs last.

Note: It's best practice to turn in the cover material with overlapping side tabs because the corners are less likely to come apart or get worn out with use.

8. Prepare the endpapers by cutting the card stock paper in half widthwise so that each sheet measures 5½ x 8½ inches (14 x 21.6 cm). Place the endpapers on the inner covers to determine the sizing. Aim for a ⅛ inch (3 mm) cover trim around the endpapers. For the back cover, you may choose to trim the short edge of the endpaper by ⅛ inch (3 mm). For the front cover, the endpaper should not cover the hinge. Place the endpaper by the hinge overlapping the book cloth slightly and measure ⅛ inch (3 mm) from the fore edge of the cover. Mark this measurement on the long edge of the endpaper and trim to size.

9. Finish the covers by attaching the endpapers onto both boards, starting with the back cover. Working on a clean waste sheet, brush a thin layer of glue onto a sheet of endpaper. Place it centered on the inner back cover board. Press with your hands and use the bone folder to rub on the endpaper, moving from the center outward. Repeat this step for the remaining cover. Use the edge of the folder to slightly score the hinge gap on the front cover. Lay the covers flat to dry for at least 20 minutes. Alternatively, you can lightly press the boards with weights on top to ensure they dry flat.

## Punching the Holes

This is where the "stab" part of this binding comes in. The quickest way is to drill holes using a power drill while the book is clamped. A hand tool that you can use is a Japanese screw punch. Feel free to take these routes if you have the tools. Otherwise, we are going to punch 4 holes with an awl, which will require some strength and patience.

10. Hold the front and back covers together and check that all the edges are flush and aligned. Set the front cover aside and position the back cover with the endpaper facing up. Draw a light pencil line ½ inch (1.3 cm) from the spine edge. Line up the ruler on the pencil line. Mark two points on the line, 1 inch (2.5 cm) from the top and bottom edges. Then mark two more points in between, spaced 1¼ inches (3.2 cm) apart for a total of four marks.

Upgrade Your Toolbox: The Japanese screw punch is a nifty little hand tool for punching holes of various sizes. It has a spring mechanism that helps relieve stress on the wrist when punching. It's useful for punching clean holes into thick material like boards and multiple sheets of paper, so it's perfect for stab binding!

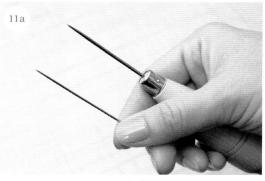

11. Compare the awl needle with the sewing needle. The awl should be slightly thicker than the sewing needle. Adequately sized holes will make the sewing process easier. If necessary, you can size down the needle and thread thicknesses. Punch holes into the back cover at the 4 pencil marks. Since the book board is thick, you'll have to use some muscle to twist the awl into the cover to create the holes. Push the awl from the front side to the back side of the cover, so that extra board material will bulge on the inside.

12. Slide the front cover under the back cover so that the book cloth sides are facing one another and the spine edges are on the same side. Make sure all the edges are flush and anchor the covers down with your non-dominant hand. Mark the holes onto the front cover by punching through the holes of the back cover with the awl. You should see small pinholes in the front cover. Repeat this process if the holes are not visible enough. Twist the awl through all four holes of the front cover from the front side through to the back side.

13. The cover holes may have some bulging from the board material being pushed through. With one end of the bone folder, rub and press the bulges flat. Erase the pencil marks on the back cover (optional).

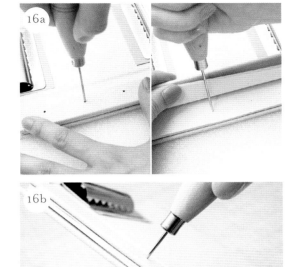

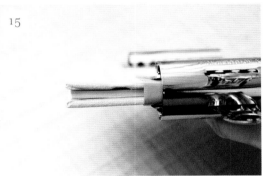

14. Place the stack of writing or sketch paper in between the front and back covers, making sure the papers are centered between the head and tail, and slightly forward from the spine edge. All the papers should be flush, with an even cover overhang around the head, tail and fore edge of the pages, about ⅛ inch (3 mm). Getting the desired alignment can take some time.

15. Using the bulldog or binder clips and clean scrap paper, clamp the book at the head and tail, leaving the holes and hinge exposed. The scrap paper is intended for protecting the book from the clips.

16. With the awl, punch holes into the pages through the holes of the front cover. Use a piece of foam or corrugated cardboard under the holes if you need the lift. It's difficult to punch through all the sheets at once, so work through the top few layers and then lift those sheets to expose unpunched paper. You may need to use a twisting motion to get deeper, being careful to not shift the papers out of alignment. Keep punching holes through a few sheets at a time until you reach the back cover. Twist the awl through each hole from front cover to back cover to ensure the holes are large enough for the needle and thread to pass through. Take your time with this step.

Note: The awl may get stuck in the papers! Use the flat surface of the metal ruler to push the needle point back out.

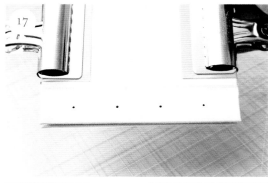

## Sewing

17. Put the needle through the holes to check that they are wide enough to sew through. Re-punch the holes if necessary. You can use any needle, but I find that straight needles are more effective for stab binding. Each hole will now be referred to as a sewing station. Sewing stations are numbered 1 to 4 going from left to right with the spine facing you.

18. Measure and cut thread that is four and a half times the length of the book spine. Thread the needle on one end and pull it through 1 to 2 inches (2.5 to 5 cm). Fold the thread and press it flat with your fingers.

19. Start sewing up through station 2 from the bottom to the top of the book and leave a 2-inch (5-cm) tail.

20. Bring the needle around the spine edge and sew up through station 2 again, being careful not to pull the thread out. It may be a tight fit for the needle, so wiggle the needle as you pull it through. Wear rubber or silicone thimbles for gripping the needle if necessary. Pull the thread taut.

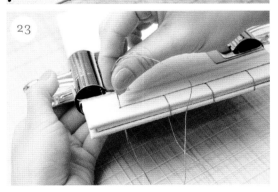

21. Sew down through station 3 to the bottom. Bring the needle around the spine edge and sew down through station 3 again. Pull the thread taut.

22. Sew up through station 4 to the top. Bring the needle around the spine edge and sew up through station 4 again. Then bring the needle around the tail edge and sew back into station 4. Pull the thread taut. Shift the position of the stitches into alignment.

23. Sew down through station 3 to the bottom, then up through station 2 to the top, and down through station 1 to the bottom.

24. Bring the needle around the spine edge and sew down through station 1 to the bottom. Then bring the needle around the head edge and sew back into station 1. Pull the thread taut and shift the stitches into alignment.

25. Your working thread should meet the starting end of the thread. Tie a double overhand knot with both ends as close to a sewing station as possible. Cut off the excess thread. Press the knot flat with the bone folder and tuck in the thread ends.

## Making a Soft Cover

To make a stab-bound book with soft covers, simply use two sheets of card stock paper the same size as the pages, with the grain running parallel to the spine. For sturdier covers, create folded edges at the fore edge, like the soft cover in Perfect Binding (page 38).

After trying the classic 4-hole sewing method, try these stitch variations. I used 8.5 x 11 inch (21.6 x 27.9 cm) paper for these notebooks with the short edge as the spine. For each stitch variation, there are 4 main holes on the top row that are 1 inch (2.5 cm) from the spine edge (see images on the next page). There is a second row of holes that are ½ inch (1.3 cm) from the spine edge, halfway between the top row and the spine. Start sewing through station 2 of the top row from the bottom and follow the numbers indicating each time you pass through a hole. Consecutive numbers mean that you will need to bring the needle around the spine, head or tail edges and re-enter the same hole.

For Hemp Leaf Binding, complete Noble Binding and continue on to number 21.

## Noble Binding

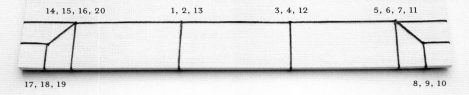

## Hemp Leaf Binding

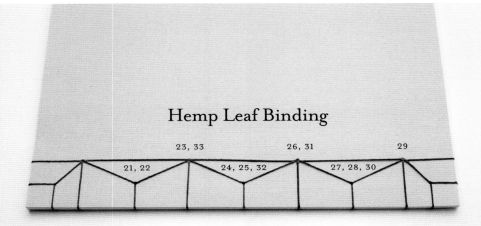

## Tortoise Shell Binding

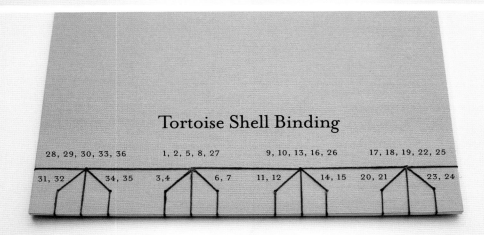

## Long Stitch with Cloth Tapes
### *Ribbon Sketchbook*

- - - - - - - - - - - - - - - - - - - - - - - - - - - - - - - - - - - - - - - - - - - - - - - - - - -

*This book structure is a charming way to make a small lay-flat sketchbook. It features French links sewn on tapes, which are joined with the covers and function as the hinges. The tapes are also used as the book closure. Traditionally, sewing on linen tapes is a method of adding extra support to heavier text blocks.*

*For this exposed spine binding, I used plush velvet ribbons as the tapes. You can use an alternative sturdy ribbon, such as cotton twill, or even book cloth made into tapes. I recommend making smaller books with this structure, as the tape hinges can only support lightweight books.*

- - - - - - - - - - - - - - - - - - - - - - - - - - - - - - - - - - - - - - - - - - - - - - - - - - -

**Difficulty:** ★ ★

**New skills:** sewing on tapes, altering cover boards, working with decorative paper, long stitch variation

- - - - - - - - - - - - - - - - - - - - - - - - - - - - - - - - - - - - - - - - - - - - - - - - - - -

## materials

- 30 sheets of 6 x 9 inch (15.2 x 22.9 cm) sketch paper, 60–80lb (90–120gsm), grain short
- Strip of stiff paper cut to 6 inches (15.2 cm) in length and 2–3 inches (5–7.6 cm) in width
- ⅞-inch (2.2-cm) wide velvet ribbon, at least 32 inches (81.3 cm) long
- Waxed linen thread, any gauge
- 2 sheets of 4⅝ x 6¼ inch (11.7 x 15.9 cm) book board, grain long
- Waste sheets for gluing
- 2 sheets of 6¼ x 7¾ inch (15.9 x 19.7 cm) decorative paper, grain long
- PVA glue
- Clean scrap paper
- 2 sheets of 4½ x 6 inch (11.4 x 15.2 cm) card stock paper, 80–100lb (216–270gsm) cover weight, grain long
- Moisture barrier sheets

## tools

- Bone folder
- Ruler
- Pencil
- Cutting mat
- Awl
- Scissors
- Needle
- Utility knife
- Square card or square ruler
- Glue brush
- Large bulldog or binder clip
- Lighter or wax for sealing ribbon edge

## Making the Text Block

I. Start by folding five sheets of sketch paper in half, with the short edges meeting each other. Crease the fold with the bone folder. Flip the folded papers vertically and crease the fold one more time. This is the first signature, which should measure 4½ x 6 inches (11.4 x 15.2 cm). Make five more signatures like this with the remaining sheets.

2. The strip of stiff paper, which is the same length as the signatures, will be the guide for punching holes. There will be six holes in total, two for each tape. With ruler and pencil, measure and mark the following points on the long edge of the stiff paper: ½ inch (1.3 cm), 1½ inches (3.8 cm), 2½ inches (6.4 cm), 3½ inches (8.9 cm), 4½ inches (11.4 cm), and 5½ inches (14 cm). The holes are ⅛ inch (3 mm) wider than the width of the tapes. The image shows the spacing between the marks.

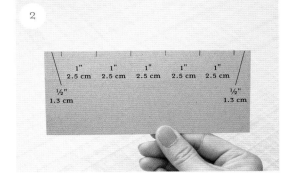

2

1"
2.5 cm   1"
2.5 cm   1"
2.5 cm   1"
2.5 cm   1"
2.5 cm

½"
1.3 cm                              ½"
1.3 cm

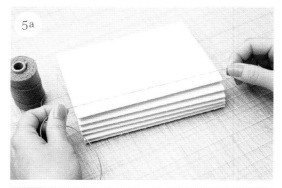

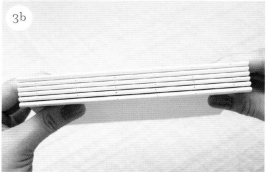

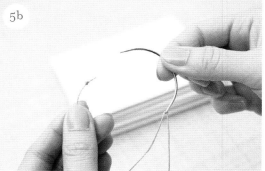

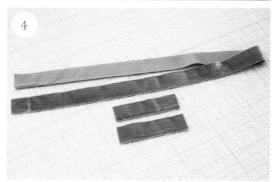

## Sewing on Tapes

The text block will be sewn with three pieces of ribbon along the spine, with French links as a decorative and supportive stitch. Each hole in the signatures will be referred to as a sewing station. Sewing stations are numbered 1 to 6 on the spine, going from left to right.

3. Working on the cutting mat, open the first signature and place the punching guide up against the fold. Hold the awl at a 45-degree angle and punch holes through the fold at each point marked on the guide. Repeat this for all six signatures. Hold the signatures together and check that the holes are aligned.

4. Prepare the ribbon by cutting it with your scissors into the following lengths: two pieces measuring 3 inches (7.6 cm) and one piece measuring at least 26 inches (66 cm).

5. Measure and cut waxed linen thread that is seven times the length of the signatures. Tie a double overhand knot on one end and thread the other end through a needle.

6a

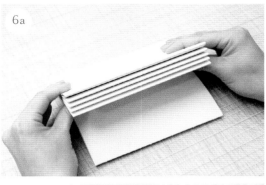

6b

7

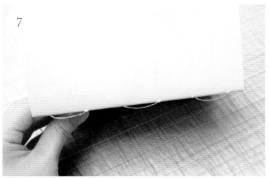

8a

6. Position the signatures with their spines facing you. Pick up all but the bottom signature and flip them over in front of you. This is important because it is easy to mix up the alignment of the holes if the signatures are placed randomly. With the needle and thread, starting from the inside of the signature, sew out through the 6th (rightmost) station and pull the thread all the way to the knot.

7. Sew in through station 5, out through station 4, in through station 3, out through station 2, and in through station 1. Keep the stitches fairly loose to insert the tapes in the next step.

8. Slip the two shorter tapes in through the outer stitches (between stations 1 and 2 and stations 5 and 6) of the signature, positioning the ribbon so that the stitch lands on the middle of the tape. Slip the long tape through the middle stitch between stations 3 and 4.

8b

Pull the working thread taut to the left, in the direction of sewing to avoid tearing the paper. The tapes will flop around as you sew and will need to be handled methodically throughout the sewing process. Sew out through station 2 to the outside to prepare for adding a new signature.

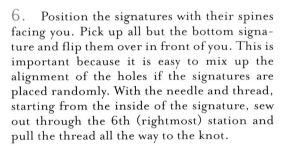

## Even-Numbered Signature

9. Pick up a new signature and flip it onto the working book. At a glance, match the alignment of the sewing stations. Hold the signatures together with your non-dominant hand to prevent shifting. Sew through station 2 of the new signature to the inside. You will now be working with the stations of this signature. Sew through station 1 to the outside. Create a French Link Stitch by sewing up behind the stitch directly below, being careful to not snag the ribbon with the needle. Sew in through station 2.

10. Sew through station 3 to the outside and create a French link by sewing up behind the stitch directly below. Sew through station 4 to the inside.

11. Sew out through station 5 and create a French link by sewing up behind the stitch directly below. Sew in through station 6 and pull taut towards the right. Sew through station 5 to the outside.

12a

12b

## Odd-Numbered Signature

12. Pick up a new signature and flip it onto the working book. At a glance, match the alignment of the sewing stations. Sew in through station 5 of the new signature. You will now be working with the stations of this signature. Sew out through station 6 to the outside, then create a French link by sewing up behind the stitch directly below. Sew through station 5 to the inside.

13. Sew through station 4 to the outside and create a French link by sewing up behind the stitch directly below. Sew through station 3 to the inside.

14. Sew through station 2 to the outside and create a French link by sewing up behind the stitch directly below. Sew in through station 1 and pull taut towards the left. Sew through station 2 to the outside.

14a

14b

16

15. To sew on the 4th signature, follow steps 9 through 11. To sew on the 5th signature, follow steps 12 through 14. For the 6th signature, follow steps 9 through 11, but do not sew through station 5 to the outside at the last step.

16. Complete the sewing by making a half hitch knot (page 23) on the inside of the signature. Cut off the excess thread.

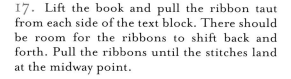

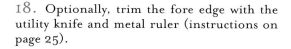

17. Lift the book and pull the ribbon taut from each side of the text block. There should be room for the ribbons to shift back and forth. Pull the ribbons until the stitches land at the midway point.

18. Optionally, trim the fore edge with the utility knife and metal ruler (instructions on page 25).

## Making the Covers

Using a board thickness of at least 0.08 inch (2 mm) is important for making recessed channels where the ribbons will be laid in.

19. Holding the text block upright with the spine edge down, place a book board against the right side of the text block, under the ribbons. Center the text block between the head and tail of the board. With a pencil, indicate the placement of the ribbons by tracing the width of each ribbon onto the board. Gently pull the ribbon to remove any slack when doing so. There should be six marks total. Draw an arrow pointing up to indicate the head of the book. This will be the back cover.

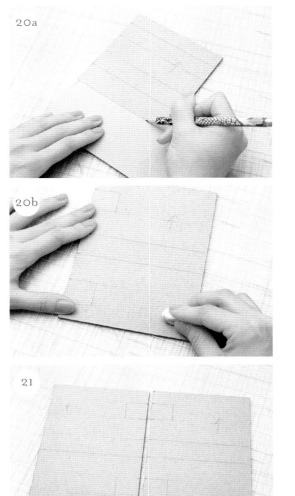

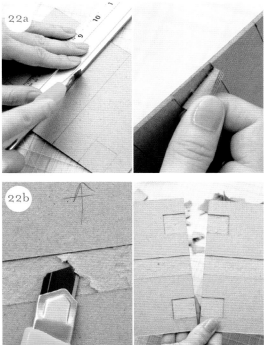

20. Use a square card or square ruler to draw lines across the width of the cover board at all six points. Then measure and mark 1 inch (2.5 cm) on the top and bottom edges from the left side. Line up the ruler along those points and draw vertical lines between lines 1 and 2, and lines 5 and 6. Erase the pencil marks beyond the vertical lines. The 1-inch (2.5-cm) space is where the top and bottom ribbons will be attached.

21. Place the front cover next to the back cover with the inner edges touching. Using the back cover as a guide, mark the channel spacing onto the front cover. Draw an arrow pointing up, indicating the head of the book. Repeat step 20 to draw the channel lines on the front cover, with the 1-inch (2.5-cm) spacing on the right-side edge.

22. With a ruler and utility knife, score the lines of the channels by making two cuts per line with medium pressure. Be careful to not cut all the way through. Create a recessed channel by peeling about half of the board thickness layer by layer, or less if you're using a thinner ribbon. Use the blade to lift the fibers. Make sure the channels are peeled evenly. Lay the ribbon in the channel to test the depth, as the goal is for ribbon to be flush with the board. Repeat for the remaining cover.

23a

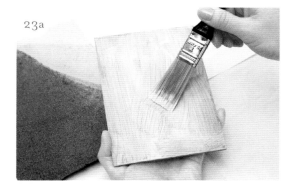

23b

23c

24

23. Cover your workspace with waste sheets for gluing. Pick up the decorative paper for the front cover. Note the pattern direction and make sure it's upright when it's glued down. Brush a thin layer of glue onto the front cover board and place it centered onto the decorative paper, with an even trim on all the edges. Flip the cover over and press with your palms. Trim the cover paper if necessary, to create tabs that are about ¾ inch (1.9 cm). Gently rub on the decorative paper outward from the center using the length of the bone folder to smooth out any bubbles or wrinkles.

24. Flip the cover over. Cut each corner of the decorative paper at a 45-degree angle, leaving about ⅛ inch (3 mm) of excess. This tiny space is important for the next step of neatly wrapping the cover material around the book board, also known as turn-ins. The excess space should be slightly wider than the thickness of the board.

Note: You may find that each kind of decorative paper responds differently to glue. Generally, lighter weight papers are stretchier when wet but mold around corners and edges really well, and heavier weight papers can be easier to work with but will add some bulk. As you explore, you'll find your favorite papers to work with.

25a

25b

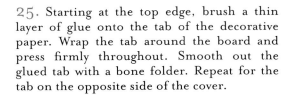

26a

26b

25. Starting at the top edge, brush a thin layer of glue onto the tab of the decorative paper. Wrap the tab around the board and press firmly throughout. Smooth out the glued tab with a bone folder. Repeat for the tab on the opposite side of the cover.

26. Brush a thin layer of glue onto the tab at the fore edge. Use the bone folder to tuck in and press the corner bits flat. Wrap the tab over the book board's edge. Use the edge of the bone folder to press the paper into the recessed space.

27. Brush a thin layer of glue onto the remaining tab. Use the bone folder to tuck in and press the corner bits flat. Position your thumb at the channels and wrap the tab over the board edge. Then wrap and press on the rest of the tab. Use the edge of the bone folder to press the decorative paper into the recessed channels.

27

28. Repeat steps 23 through 27 to apply decorative paper onto the back cover.

Note: It's best practice to turn in the cover material with overlapping side tabs because the corners are less likely to come apart or get worn out with use.

29a

29b

30

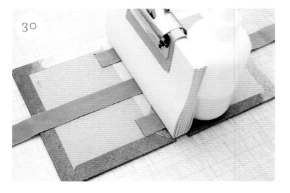

## Joining the Text Block and Covers

The ribbons make up the hinges of this book. This book structure is naturally slightly floppy, so I've extended the ribbon to use as a closure at the fore edge. To join the text block and covers, the ribbons are glued into the recessed channels of the covers, then secured with the endpapers.

29. Using a bulldog or binder clip and clean scrap paper, clamp the fore edge of the text block to keep the pages together. Hold the text block upright with the spine edge down. Place the back cover on the right side of the text block, lining up the channels with the ribbons. Trim the top and bottom ribbons to match the length of the recessed channels. Brush a thin layer of glue into all three channels and lay the tapes into place. There should be no slack at the hinges. Briefly close the cover to check that the spine edge is flush with the text block spine. Continue to hold the text block upright as you press the tapes down into the channels. Wipe away any glue overflow.

Tip: use an object to prop up the text block to free your hand for gluing Use small weights to add pressure on the tapes for better adhesion.

30. Repeat step 29 to join the front cover. Be careful to not shift the covers out of place while the glue is still wet. Optionally, wait about 15 minutes for the glue to set before attaching the endpapers.

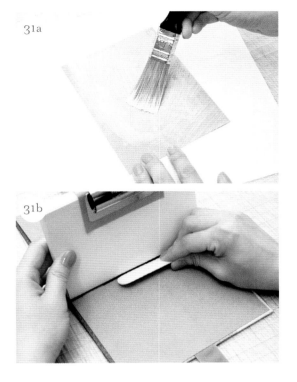

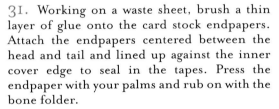

31. Working on a waste sheet, brush a thin layer of glue onto the card stock endpapers. Attach the endpapers centered between the head and tail and lined up against the inner cover edge to seal in the tapes. Press the endpaper with your palms and rub on with the bone folder.

32. Lay the book open flat to dry if the text block can stand on its spine, or dry the book closed with moisture barrier sheets in between the inner covers and text block.

33. Cut the middle ribbon to a desired length. To prevent the ribbon from fraying, seal the edges with a lighter. If the ribbon is made of natural material, dip the edge in melted wax to seal it. To finish the book, tie the ribbons together.

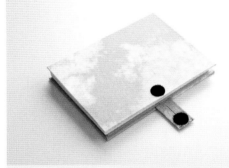

Velcro variation: Alternatively, you can apply a Velcro fastener by trimming the tape on the front cover flush with the fore edge. Then shorten the tape on the back cover to wrap around to the front cover where the closure is installed.

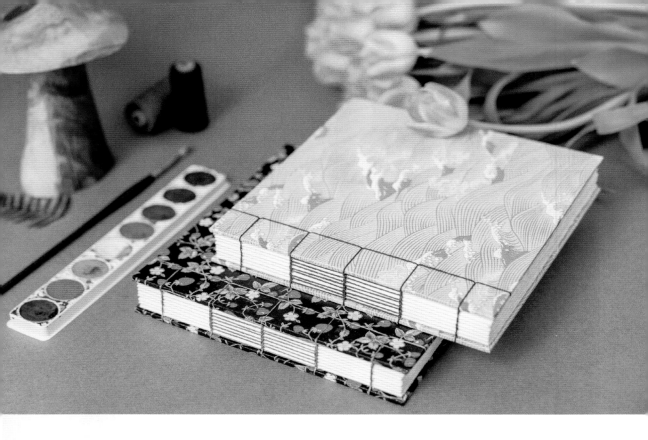

# Coptic Stitch Binding
## *Lay-Flat Sketchbook*

- - - - - - - - - - - - - - - - - - - - - - - - - - - - - - - - - - - - - - - - - - - - -

*Books made with Coptic stitch binding have an exposed spine and can lay flat. I fell in love with the countless variations of the spine stitching that can be used to customize a book with this design. I've used Coptic stitch to make bullet journals, mixed media sketchbooks and watercolor sketchbooks. Coptic stitch is especially excellent for sketchbooks that hold wet media because they can lay flat during a painting session and allow for easy drying. This is one of the oldest binding methods originating from Egypt as early as 200 AD.*

*This project is a square sketchbook made with 100 percent cotton watercolor paper. Feel free to adapt these instructions with the paper of your choice or make a different size. You can use decorative paper or book cloth as the cover material.*

- - - - - - - - - - - - - - - - - - - - - - - - - - - - - - - - - - - - - - - - - - - - -

**Difficulty:** ★ ★ ★

**New skills:** tearing heavyweight paper, exposed spine sewing,
joining threads, sewing on cover boards, decorative stitching

- - - - - - - - - - - - - - - - - - - - - - - - - - - - - - - - - - - - - - - - - - - - -

## materials

- 2 square sheets of 7¾ x 7¾ inch (19.7 x 19.7 cm) book board, 0.08–0.12 inch (2–3 mm) thick
- 2 square sheets of 9¼ x 9¼ inch (23.5 x 23.5 cm) decorative paper
- 2 square sheets of 7½ x 7½ inch (19 x 19 cm) card stock paper, 80–100lb (216–270gsm) cover weight
- Waste sheets
- PVA glue
- 4 sheets (22 x 30 inch [56 x 76 cm]) of watercolor paper
- Strip of stiff paper cut to 7½ inches (19 cm) in length and 2–3 inches (5–8 cm) in width
- Waxed linen thread, any gauge

## tools

- Pencil
- Glue brush
- Bone folder
- Utility knife
- Metal ruler
- Cutting mat
- Awl
- Scissors
- Needle, curved needle preferred

## Making the Covers

1.    Start by using a pencil to mark the direction of the paper grain (page 20) on the sheets of book board, decorative paper and card stock endpaper. Draw an arrow pointing to the head of the book on the back side of all six pieces of cover material. When the papers are glued together, be sure to match the paper grain going in the same direction to prevent warping and to ensure that the covers remain flat.

2.    Let's cover the book boards with decorative paper. Lay out a waste sheet on your workspace and grab the first book board. With a glue brush, spread a thin layer of glue on the front side of the board (the side without the arrow). Match the paper grain by ensuring the arrows of both pieces point in the same direction and place the board in the center of a sheet of decorative paper so that there is an even trim of paper around the edges. Press down gently, then flip the cover over so that the decorative side is facing up.

3. Rub on the decorative paper using the length of a bone folder with medium pressure. Gently rub outward from the center to smooth out any bubbles or wrinkles. You can also use your fingers and palms to press out the bubbles.

4. Flip the cover over. Cut each corner of the decorative paper at a 45-degree angle, leaving about ⅛ inch (3 mm) of excess. This tiny space should be slightly wider than the thickness of the board, and is important for the next step of neatly wrapping the cover material around the book board, also known as turn-ins.

5. Starting at the top edge of the cover, brush a thin layer of glue onto the tab of decorative paper. Wrap the tab around the board and press firmly throughout. Smooth out the glued tab with a bone folder. Repeat for the tab on the opposite side of this cover.

Note: When decorative paper is glued onto one side of book board, the board will start to bow outwards due to paper pull. Generally, gluing endpapers on the other side should balance out the pulling force on the book board, straightening it out when it's dry.

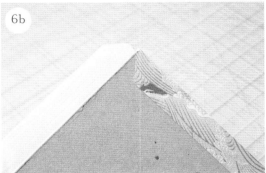

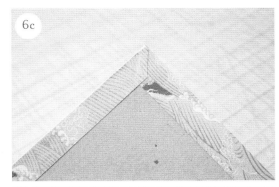

6. Let's turn in the side tabs. Brush glue onto one of the remaining two tabs. Use the bone folder to tuck in and press the corner bits flat. Wrap the tab over the book board's edge. Repeat for the last side tab.

7. Cover the other book board with decorative paper by following steps 2 through 6.

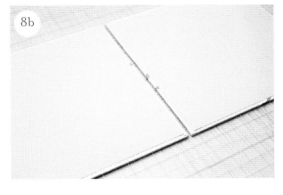

8. Finish the covers by gluing the card stock endpapers onto both boards. Remember to match the grain direction with the arrows pointing in the same direction. Rub them on with the bone folder from the center moving outward. Lay the covers flat to dry. Alternatively, you can lightly press the boards with weights on top to ensure they dry flat.

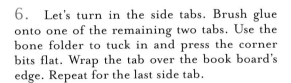

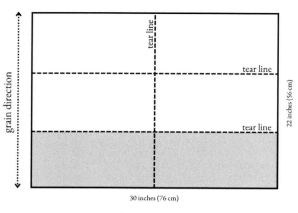

short grain paper

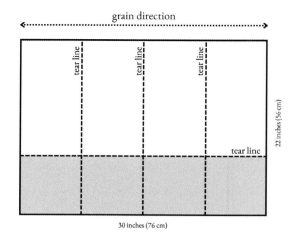

long grain paper

## Preparing the Signatures

To make this sketchbook, I made eight signatures by tearing four 22 x 30-inch (56 x 76–cm) sheets of 100-percent-cotton cold-press watercolor paper by Fabriano® Artistico, which has a short grain running widthwise. Each signature consists of two 7½ x 15–inch (19 x 38–cm) sheets folded in half. The 100 percent cotton watercolor paper tears nicely, and the torn page edges are a beautiful feature for the sketchbook. I've included instructions for tearing long-grain paper as well. Find out the grain of watercolor paper you're using on page 20. The grain will determine how the paper will be torn and folded for the signatures of the book. If you prefer straight edges, cut the paper with a utility knife.

9. With a pencil, mark the halfway point on the 30-inch (76-cm) edge of the watercolor sheet and draw a line down the middle. Note: some papers are manufactured slightly longer than 30 inches (76 cm), so the halfway mark may not be exactly at 15 inches (38 cm). Hold the ruler down firmly with your non-dominant hand, being careful not to shift the ruler or paper, and tear the paper against the metal edge with your dominant hand.

**Time-Saving Tip:** If you have a large cutting mat with grid lines, you can use the lines as a guide to tear the paper. Measure and mark where you'd like to tear and line up the long edge of the sheet to a horizontal line on the cutting mat. Line up the mark and the edge of the ruler along a vertical line. Use the top 3 inches (7.6 cm) of the ruler to match the vertical line of the cutting mat. Tear the sheet along the line against a metal ruler.

11

12a

12b

IO. **Short grain paper**: Stack the two half sheets together and along the 22-inch (56-cm) edge and measure two points: 7½ inches (19 cm) and 15 inches (38 cm). Mark these points and draw tear lines along the width of the top sheet. Tear both sheets together along these lines with the metal ruler. You should now have four sheets of 7½ x 15–inch (19 x 38-cm) paper and two sheets of 7 x 15–inch (17.8 x 38–cm) paper.

**Long grain paper**: Stack the two half sheets together and along the 15-inch (38-cm) edge, measure and mark the halfway point. Draw a tear line along the length of the sheet. Tear both sheets together along this line with a metal ruler. You should have four sheets of 7½ x 22–inch (19 x 56–cm) paper. Tear the sheets two at a time, to a length of 15 inches (38 cm).

II. Take a stack of two 7½ x 15–inch (19 x 38–cm) sheets and fold them in half together. Crease the fold with the bone folder. This is your first signature. Make a second signature with the remaining two 7½ x 15–inch (19 x 38–cm) sheets.

I2. Repeat steps 9 through 11 with the remaining three watercolor paper sheets to create eight signatures in total. Stack all the signatures together and place them in between the front and back covers.

Tip: Press the signatures under weights to flatten the folds further.

The sketchbook has all its main components. While the covers and signatures are still loose, flip through each piece and make sure the positioning is correct and desirable. For example, ensure the patterns on the covers are upright when flipping the book from front to back. From this point on, keep all of the pieces together and in order as you move on to punching the holes and sewing.

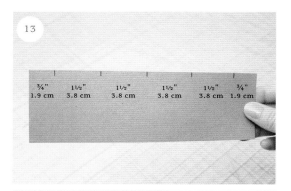

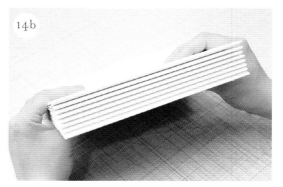

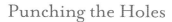

## Punching the Holes

13. The strip of stiff paper, which is the same length as the signatures, will be your guide for punching holes. Measure and mark ¾ inch (1.9 cm) on the long edge from the left and right sides. Then mark three more points spaced 1½ inches (3.8 cm) apart in between the two end points for a total of five marks.

14. Working on the cutting mat, open the top signature and place the stiff paper guide up against the fold, or the valley, of the signature. Hold the awl at a 45-degree angle and punch holes through the fold at each point marked on the guide. Pierce the paper until the needle tip is visible on the other side and do not enlarge the holes. Repeat this step for all eight signatures. Hold all the signatures together and check that the holes are aligned.

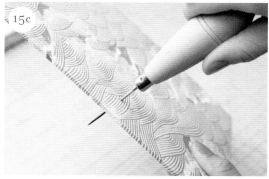

16

17a

17b

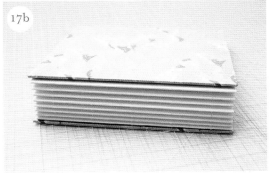

15. Draw a light pencil line across the back cover 1 inch (2.5 cm) from the spine edge of the board. Line up the bottom signature with the pencil line and center the signature between the head and tail edges of the cover. Using the awl, punch holes into the cover by following the holes of the signature. Since the book board is thick, you'll have to use some muscle to twist the awl into the cover to create the holes. Push the awl from the front side to the back side of the cover, so that the extra board material will bulge on the inside.

16. To create holes in the front cover, slide the front cover under the back cover, so that their decorative sides are facing one another and the spine edges are on the same side. Make sure all of the edges are flush. Mark the holes on the front cover by punching through the holes you made in the back cover with the awl. Twist the awl through all five holes of the front cover.

17. The cover holes may have some bulging from the board material being pushed through. With one end of the bone folder, rub and press the bulges flat so that the inside covers are more aesthetically pleasing. Erase the pencil marks.

To prepare for sewing, assemble all the pieces of the book together in the desired order, checking to make sure all of the holes line up vertically across the spine.

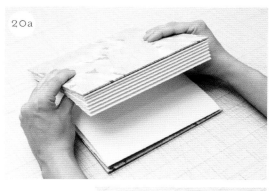

20a

20b

21a

21b

## Sewing - Coptic Stitch Binding

You are now ready to sew! The book will be sewn from back cover to front cover, and bottom to top. Each hole in the signatures and covers will now be referred to as a sewing station. Sewing stations are numbered 1 to 5 going from left to right.

18. Place the book on the desk with the spine facing you. Measure the waxed linen thread to ten times the length of the book and cut with scissors.

19. Tie a double overhand knot on one end, and thread the other end through a curved needle.

20. Pick up the front cover and seven signatures and flip them over in front of you. This is important because it is easy to mix up the alignment of the holes if the signatures are placed randomly. You will work on the back cover and remaining signature first, then add new signatures as you go along, ending with the front cover. With your needle, starting from the inside of the signature, sew out through the 5th (rightmost) station and pull the thread all the way to the knot.

21. Sew up through the adjacent hole in the cover starting from the outside. Pull the thread taut, which will line up the signature with the cover. Your working thread should be on the left of the vertical stitch you just made. Hold the book firmly together with your non-dominant hand to prevent excessive shifting.

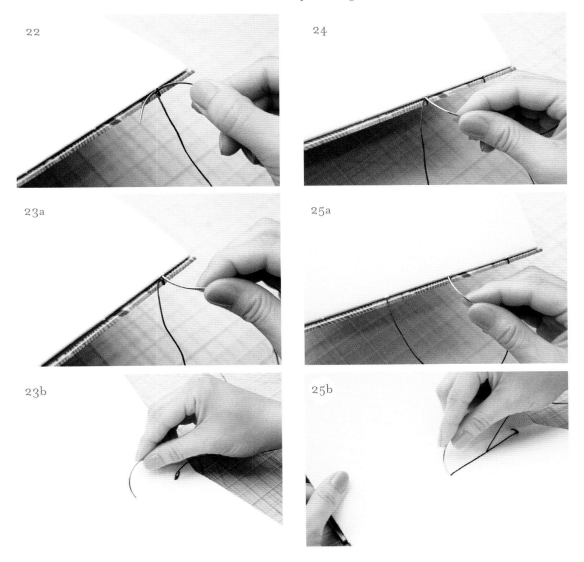

22

24

23a

25a

23b

25b

22. Sew behind the vertical stitch, bringing your needle from right to left in the space between the cover and signature. Pull taut.

23. From the outside, sew back into the 5th sewing station of the signature and then come back out through the 4th station.

24. Repeat steps 21 and 22 with station 4. Sew back into station 4. Your needle should now be on the inside of the signature.

25. Now we're going to create the ladder stitch aesthetic on the mid-spine. Sew out through station 3, then in through station 4, and back out through station 3. For this sketchbook, you're going to make a ladder stitch between sewing stations 3 and 4, and stations 2 and 3 on each signature.

28

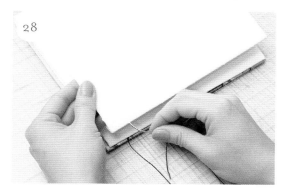

29b

29a

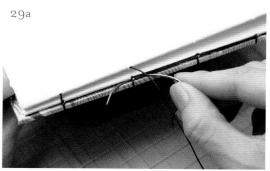
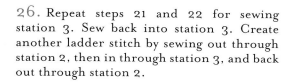

30

26. Repeat steps 21 and 22 for sewing station 3. Sew back into station 3. Create another ladder stitch by sewing out through station 2, then in through station 3, and back out through station 2.

27. Continue sewing on the cover by repeating steps 21 and 22 for station 2. Sew back into station 2 and then come back out through station 1. Repeat steps 21 and 22 for station 1. Your needle should now be on the outside of station 1.

28. To add a new signature, flip the next signature from the stack onto the working book and match the alignment of the sewing stations at a glance. Starting from the outside, sew into station 1 of the new signature. Hold the book firmly together with your non-dominant hand to prevent excessive shifting.

29. Sew out through station 2. Loop your needle behind the stitch connecting the cover and the 1st signature. You may have to open the book slightly to make room for your needle. Make sure you are not sewing under the stitch that attaches the back cover. Pull taut, then sew back into station 2.

30. Create a ladder stitch by sewing out through station 3, then in through station 2, and back out through station 3. Loop your needle behind the stitch connecting the cover and the 1st signature and pull taut. Sew back into station 3.

31

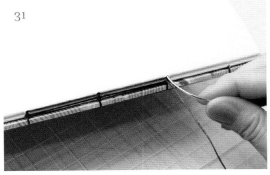

32b

32a

32c

31. Create another ladder stitch by sewing out through station 4, then in through station 3, and back out through station 4. Loop your needle behind the stitch connecting the cover and the 1st signature and pull taut. Sew back into station 4. Your needle should now be on the inside of the signature.

32. Sew out through station 5 and create a kettle stitch (page 23) with the stitch directly below. For Coptic books, make a kettle stitch when you reach the end of every signature.

To add odd-numbered signatures, start in sewing station 5 and end at station 1. To add even-numbered signatures, start in sewing station 1 and end at station 5. Create ladder stitches between stations 2 and 3, and stations 3 and 4. Continue to add new signatures until you've reached the last one as that signature will be sewn along with the front cover. Be sure to loop stitches directly below the new signature. You'll start to see vertical chains form on the 3rd and subsequent signatures.

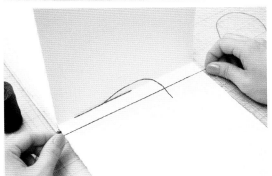

Note: After finishing signature 4, you will be running low on thread. When you're down to your last few inches of thread (minimum 2 inches [5 cm]), make sure the thread is on the inside of a signature, and somewhere in between sewing stations 1 and 5. Measure and cut another piece of thread that is ten times the length of the book. Connect the ends of the old thread and the new thread together with a weaver's knot (page 24).

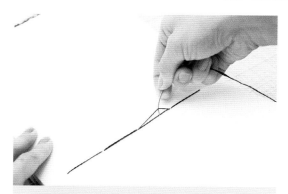

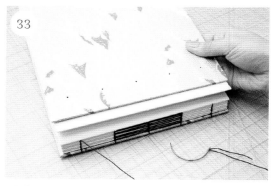

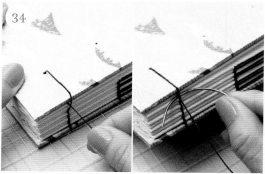

Tip: You can increase thread tension at any point of the sewing by using your needle to pull the previous stitches taut from inside the current signature you're working on. Be sure to not pull the thread with enough force to rip the paper along the fold. Coptic book spines are naturally slightly loose, and the stitching should allow the spine (the folded edges of the signatures) to be aligned and square. If the spine is curved inward, the sewing tension is too tight.

33. After you finish sewing on the 7th signature, add the final signature and front cover to the book. It's tricky to get the thread tension right at this next stage, so take your time and remember to not over-tighten stitches.

34. Sew down through station 1 of the cover from the outside. The thread should be on the left side of the new vertical stitch. Pull the thread taut while aligning the spine. Loop your needle behind the stitch between the 7th and 8th signatures.

35. Now sew into station 1 of the 8th signature, then out through station 2. This stage requires some coordinated handling of the loose pieces with your non-dominant hand while you sew.

36. Loop your needle behind the stitch connecting the 6th and 7th signatures and then sew the needle down through station 2 of the cover. Pull the thread through the spine on the left side of the stitch and close the cover. Pull taut while ensuring the spine remains in alignment.

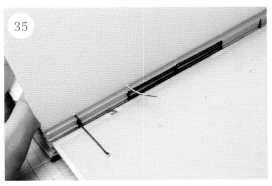

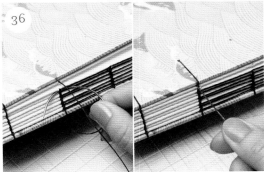

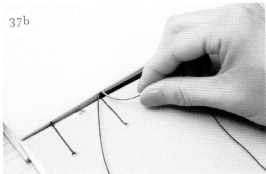

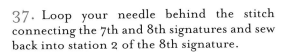

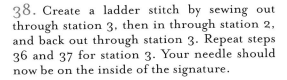

37. Loop your needle behind the stitch connecting the 7th and 8th signatures and sew back into station 2 of the 8th signature.

38. Create a ladder stitch by sewing out through station 3, then in through station 2, and back out through station 3. Repeat steps 36 and 37 for station 3. Your needle should now be on the inside of the signature.

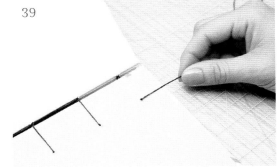

39. Create another ladder stitch by sewing out through station 4, then in through station 3, and back out through station 4. Repeat steps 36 and 37 for station 4, then come back out through station 5. For station 5, repeat step 36 only. Your needle should now be on the inside between the cover and 8th signature.

40. For this step you'll be working with the stations on the cover to create the decorative stitching that resembles stab binding. Pull the thread to the right-side edge of the spine, bring it around to the front and sew back into station 5. Sew out through station 4, in through station 3, out through station 2, and in through station 1. Bring the thread up over the top edge of the book and back in through station 1. Weave through all sewing stations until you are on the inside of station 5.

41. Bring the needle through the spine on the left side of station 5's stitch. Create a kettle stitch with the stitch connecting the 7th and 8th signatures and sew in through station 5 of the 8th signature.

42. Using your needle, pull the decorative cover stitches taut starting with the stitch wrapping the bottom edge of the cover, then pull the stitch between stations 3 and 4, then between stations 1 and 2, then the top edge, then between stations 2 and 3, then between stations 4 and 5, then the stitch at station 5 on the inside cover, and finally pull the working thread on the inside of the 8th signature.

Note: You may have to temporarily unthread the needle for this step.

43. With the book open to the middle of the 8th signature, rethread the needle and bring it under the stitch between stations 4 and 5. Tie a half hitch knot through the loose loop you just created. Make one more knot like this and pull taut. Cut the excess thread.

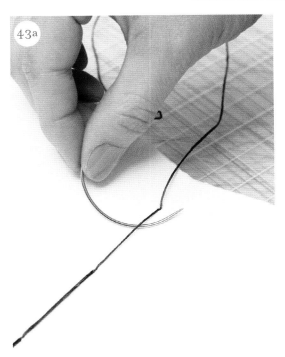

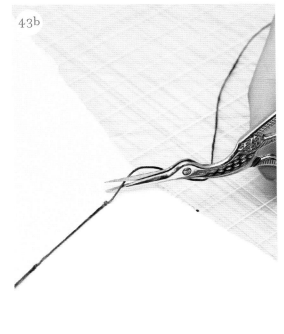

44. Close the book and admire your work! Check your thread tension. If it's too loose, you may need to tighten more often as you sew. With the right amount of tension, it is normal for the book to not close completely as the sewing is still fresh. You can weigh down or lightly press your book for at least half a day so that the binding can relax before using it. The binding will also relax naturally as the book is used over time. With any exposed spine bindings, it is also normal for the signatures to shift or have some wiggle room. Even if the binding loosens, the book will not come apart if you used strong thread.

Closure option: I like to use a journal band (page 175) to wrap the book. It's a great way to complete the book design and provide extra support for the spine stitching.

# Long Stitch with Quarter Binding
## *Photo Albums and Scrapbooks*

- - - - - - - - - - - - - - - - - - - - - - - - - - - - - - - - - - - - - - - - - - - - - - - - - -

*This is my go-to binding to make photo albums and scrapbooks. A hardcover long stitch book offers adequate support and spacing in between the pages for photos and scrapbook ephemera. The sewing demonstrated in this project is the most standard style of long stitch and is complemented by quarter binding, an elegant way to use two different cover materials. The spine is covered in book cloth, and the rest of the cover is adorned with decorative paper.*

*In this project, I show you how to make a photo album that holds 4" x 6" (10.16 x 15.24 cm) photos. Use acid-free, archival quality materials to preserve the photos. Feel free to adapt these instructions to make an album for a different size photo. Switch out the stiffened spine for a board spine and this binding would be great for making a journal or sketchbook.*

- - - - - - - - - - - - - - - - - - - - - - - - - - - - - - - - - - - - - - - - - - - - - - - - - -

**Difficulty:** ★ ★

**New skills:** making a round stiffened spine, adding spacers between pages, quarter binding

- - - - - - - - - - - - - - - - - - - - - - - - - - - - - - - - - - - - - - - - - - - - - - - - - -

## materials

- 1 strip of 4¼ x 7½ inch (10.8 x 19 cm) book cloth
- 2 strips of 1⅛ x 5¾ inch (2.9 x 14.6 cm) card stock paper, 80–100lb (216–270gsm) cover weight, grain long
- Waste sheets for gluing
- PVA glue
- 2 sheets of 5¾ x 7½ inch (14.6 x 19 cm) book board, 0.08-inch (2 mm) thick, grain short
- 2 sheets of 7¼ x 7¼ inch (18.4 x 18.4 cm) decorative paper
- 1 strip of 2½ x 5½ inch (6.4 x 14 cm) endpaper, medium weight preferred, grain short
- 2 sheets of 5½ x 7¼ inch (14 x 18.4 cm) endpaper, medium weight preferred, grain short (this should be the same endpaper as the above strip)
- 8 sheets of 8½ x 11 inch (21.6 x 27.9 cm) card stock paper, 80–100lb (216–270gsm) cover weight, grain long
- Waxed linen thread, any gauge

## tools

- Ruler
- Pencil and eraser
- Glue brush
- Bone folder
- ¼-inch (6-mm) spacer
- ¾-inch (1.9-cm) spacer
- Cutting mat
- Utility knife or rotary cutter
- Fabric pen for marking book cloth (optional)
- Scissors
- 1-inch (2.5-cm) spacer
- Artist tape or washi tape
- Awl
- Needle

## Making the Covers

The covers will be made with quarter binding, where the spine and hinges are connected by book cloth, and the rest of the boards will be covered with decorative paper. Since you will be sewing into the spine stiffener, using a heavier weight card stock paper is ideal for the spine.

I.    Start by checking that the book cloth edges are straight and square. Trim the edges if needed. On the paper side of the book cloth, use a ruler and pencil to mark the midway point on each short edge with a pencil. Draw a line down the middle, connecting the points. Draw a midline along the length of one strip of card stock paper as well. This will be the spine stiffener.

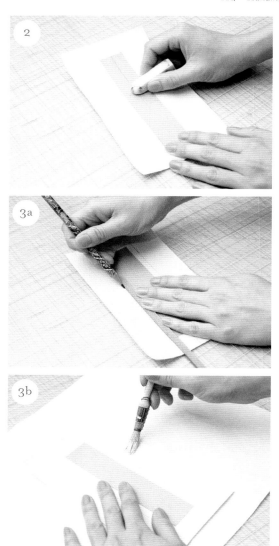

2.   Cover your workspace with a waste sheet. Brush a thin layer of glue onto the blank side of the spine stiffener and attach it centered on the strip of book cloth, aligning the pencil lines. Flip the spine piece over and rub on the book cloth with the edge of the bone folder. Erase the pencil line on the spine stiffener.

3.   Let's attach the cover boards. Place the ¼-inch (6-mm) spacer against one side of the spine stiffener and draw a line on the book cloth to mark the hinge gap. Repeat for the other side of the spine. Remove the spacer and brush a thin layer of glue on one side of the book cloth, beyond the pencil line, leaving the hinge gap area dry. Place the first book board up to the line, making sure the head and tail are level with the spine stiffener. Press to adhere. Repeat for the remaining book board on the other side. Flip the cover over and rub on the book cloth with the bone folder.

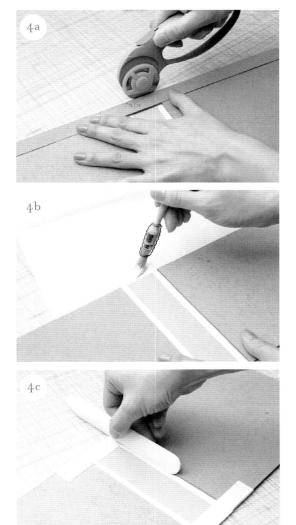

4.   Measure and mark ¾ inch (1.9 cm) from the top and bottom edges of the spine stiffener and cover boards. You can also use a spacer. Using the cutting mat and either a utility knife or rotary cutter, trim the tabs at the head and tail to ¾ inch (1.9 cm) wide. Brush glue onto the book cloth tab at the top and wrap it over the spine stiffener and cover boards. Press firmly along the tab to adhere. Smooth out the glued tab with the bone folder. Attach the book cloth tab at the bottom as well.

5.   Flip the cover over. Score the hinge by digging the tip of the bone folder into the hinge gap, pressing along the edges of the boards. There should be a groove in the book cloth along the hinges.

6.   Let's mark where the decorative paper will overlap and attach onto the book cloth edge. The narrow paper overlap seals the cloth edge to prevent it from fraying. Using a pencil or pen that will show up on the fabric, make marks at the head and tail on the book cloth, ⅛ inch (3 mm) from the cloth edge. Make a total of four marks on both the front and back covers.

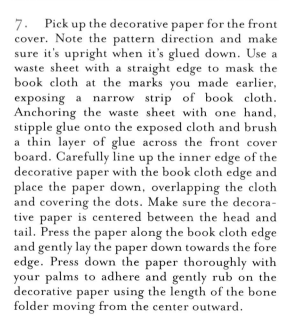

7. Pick up the decorative paper for the front cover. Note the pattern direction and make sure it's upright when it's glued down. Use a waste sheet with a straight edge to mask the book cloth at the marks you made earlier, exposing a narrow strip of book cloth. Anchoring the waste sheet with one hand, stipple glue onto the exposed cloth and brush a thin layer of glue across the front cover board. Carefully line up the inner edge of the decorative paper with the book cloth edge and place the paper down, overlapping the cloth and covering the dots. Make sure the decorative paper is centered between the head and tail. Press the paper along the book cloth edge and gently lay the paper down towards the fore edge. Press down the paper thoroughly with your palms to adhere and gently rub on the decorative paper using the length of the bone folder moving from the center outward.

8. Attach the decorative paper onto the back cover by following step 7.

9. Flip the cover over. Cut the outer four corners of the decorative paper at a 45-degree angle, leaving about ⅛ (3 mm) of excess. This tiny space is important for the next step of neatly wrapping the cover material around the book board, also known as turn-ins. The excess space should be slightly wider than the thickness of the board. Optionally, trim all the edges to ¾ inch (1.9 cm) wide for consistency.

10. Starting at the top edge of one cover, brush a thin layer of glue onto the tab of decorative paper. Wrap the tab around the board and press firmly throughout. Smooth out the glued tab with a bone folder. Repeat for the tab on the head and tail for both the front and back covers, leaving the outer side tabs to turn in last.

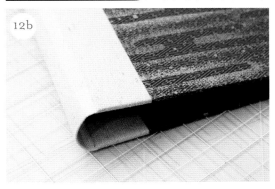

11. Brush glue onto one of the outer side tabs. Use the tip of the bone folder to tuck in and press the corner bits flat. Wrap the tab over the book board's edge. Repeat for the remaining tab.

12. Slightly round the spine stiffener by holding the cover boards with each hand and rubbing the inner spine against a straight table edge. Aim to round the stiffener evenly without causing folds. The paper grain running along the spine will help form and hold the rounded shape.

13. Finish the cover by attaching the endpapers on the inside. Working on a waste sheet, start by brushing a thin layer of glue onto the strip of spine endpaper. Carefully place it centered onto the spine stiffener with even spacing at the head and tail. Smooth out with your hands and gently press the paper into the hinge gaps and the edges of the cover boards with the bone folder. Smooth onto the cover boards.

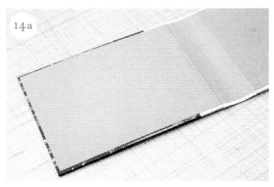

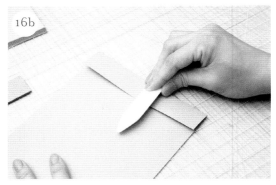

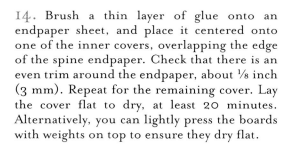

14. Brush a thin layer of glue onto an endpaper sheet, and place it centered onto one of the inner covers, overlapping the edge of the spine endpaper. Check that there is an even trim around the endpaper, about ⅛ inch (3 mm). Repeat for the remaining cover. Lay the cover flat to dry, at least 20 minutes. Alternatively, you can lightly press the boards with weights on top to ensure they dry flat.

## Preparing the Pages

Each page will have tabs in between, which function as spacers for photos and other materials to be added on the pages.

15. Use your scissors to cut all eight sheets of card stock paper in half so that you end up with sixteen sheets that measure 5½ x 8½ inches (14 x 21.6 cm).

16. Let's fold 1-inch (2.5-cm) tabs on each sheet, which will function as spacers between the pages. On one sheet of card stock, place the 1-inch spacer made of book board on the left-side edge. If you're left-handed, place the spacer on the right-side edge. Anchor the spacer down with your non-dominant hand. Using the bone folder, lift the paper and press against the spacer to make a 90-degree fold. Press and glide the edge of the bone folder along the whole length. Remove the spacer, fold the tab fully, and crease with the bone folder. Create 1-inch (2.5-cm) folded tabs for fifteen more sheets.

Note: Another way is to use the grid lines of the cutting mat and fold the paper against a ruler (image 16c).

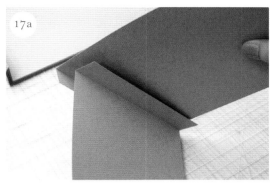

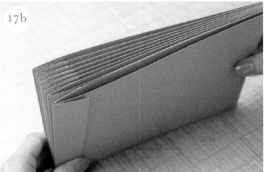

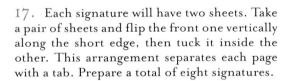

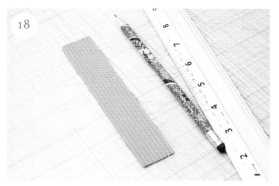

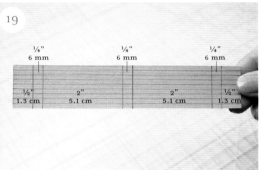

17. Each signature will have two sheets. Take a pair of sheets and flip the front one vertically along the short edge, then tuck it inside the other. This arrangement separates each page with a tab. Prepare a total of eight signatures.

Note: "Quarter binding" refers to the ratio between the area of spine material to cover material. Initially created to save on the cost of leather, now it is mainly considered as a design choice. There is also half binding, three-quarter binding and full binding.

## Punching the Holes

18. Let's create a guide for punching holes into the spine. On the stiff paper that is the same size as the spine stiffener, measure and mark eight points at the top edge that are spaced ⅛ inch (3 mm) apart. Mark the same eight points on the bottom edge. Draw vertical lines by connecting the points. These eight lines will coordinate with the eight signatures.

19. Now mark the following points on the long edge of the stiff paper: ½ inch (1.3 cm), ¾ inch (1.9 cm), 2¾ inch (7 cm), 3 inch (7.6 cm), 5 inch (12.7 cm), 5¼ inch (13.3 cm). Mark the same points on the opposite side. Draw horizontal lines across by connecting the points. Each intersection of the grid is where the holes will be punched. The image shows the spacing between the marks.

20a

20b

20c

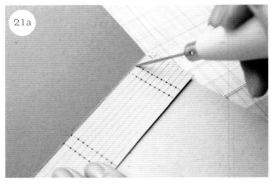

21a

21b

20. Using artist tape or washi tape, attach the punching guide over the spine on the inside, lining up the edges with the spine stiffener. Working on the cutting mat, use the awl to punch through each intersection, being careful to not shift the guide. Check the inner spine to see if the holes were punched all the way through. Gently rub the holes with the bone folder to flatten the bulging material on the outside spine. Typically, the holes would be punched on the outside but with a rounded spine, it's easier to punch from the inside. Remove the punching guide.

21. Let's punch holes into the signatures. On the long edge of the punching guide, mark two more points, ⅛ inch (3 mm) from the top and bottom edges. The distance between these points is the same length of the signatures. Open the first signature and place the punching guide up against the fold, lining up the two new outer marks with the edges of the signature. Hold the awl at a 45-degree angle and punch holes through the fold at each line on the long edge of the guide. Pierce the paper until the needle tip is visible on the other side. Repeat this step for the remaining seven signatures. Hold all of the signatures together and make sure the holes are aligned at the spine.

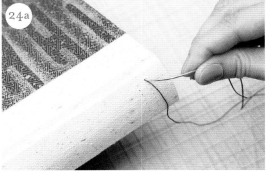

## Sewing - Long Stitch

To set up, lay the cover open on the desk with the front cover at the bottom. Place the stack of signatures within arm's reach, with the spines facing towards you. We are going to sew on one signature at a time, from front cover to back cover. The holes will be numbered as sewing stations 1 to 6, going from left to right.

22. Measure and cut waxed linen thread that is nine times the length of the spine. Tie a double overhand knot on one end. Thread the other end through a needle and pull it through 1 to 2 inches (2.5 to 5 cm). Fold the thread and press it flat with your fingers.

23. Pick up the first signature with a tab facing up. Starting from the inside of the signature, sew out through the 6th (rightmost) station and pull the thread all the way to the knot. Align the folded edge on the first row of sewing stations on the spine. Sew through station 6 of the cover to the outside spine, pulling the signature and cover to touch.

24. Hold the signature and cover in place with your non-dominant hand to prevent shifting. Sew back into the same hole of the cover and through station 6 of the signature to the inside. Pull the thread until there is a small loop on the outside spine. Be careful to not pull the thread out of the book. Hold the loop in place with a stitch holder, such as another needle.

25. Sew out through station 5 of the signature, then through station 5 of the cover to the outside. You can sew through both layers in one move as you get the hang of sewing.

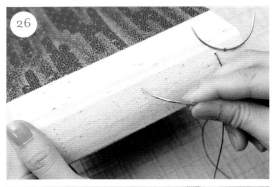

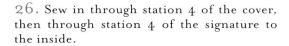

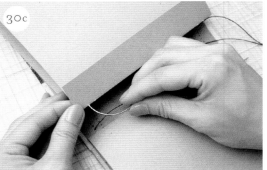

26. Sew in through station 4 of the cover, then through station 4 of the signature to the inside.

27. Sew out through station 3 of the signature, then through station 3 of the cover to the outside.

28. Sew in through station 2 of the cover, then through station 2 of the signature to the inside.

29. Sew out through station 1 of the signature, then through station 1 of the cover to the outside.

## Even-Numbered Signature

30. Let's add a new signature. Subsequent signatures will be sewn on moving further away from you. With the front cover positioned towards you, pick up a new signature and place it in front of the previous one, checking that the holes are aligned between the signatures. Sew in through station 1 of the cover at the next row of holes, then through station 1 of the new signature. Pull the thread and bring the signature and cover to touch.

Note: Each time a new signature is added, the position of the cover is reset to confirm alignment of the sewing stations. While sewing on a signature, you can maneuver your work however you need.

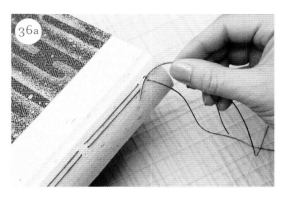

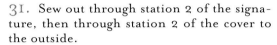

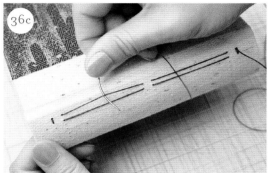

31. Sew out through station 2 of the signature, then through station 2 of the cover to the outside.

32. Sew in through station 3 of the cover, then through station 3 of the signature to the inside.

33. Sew out through station 4 of the signature, then through station 4 of the cover to the outside.

34. Sew in through station 5 of the cover, then through station 5 of the signature to the inside.

35. Sew out through station 6 of the signature, then through station 6 of the cover to the outside.

36. Carefully remove the stitch holder and sew through the loop. Pull the working thread taut.

Tip: You can increase thread tension by pulling the long stitches on the spine with the needle. Start with the first long stitch of the first signature (image 36b), then pull on the subsequent stitches by following your sewing path (image 36c) until you reach your working thread. Pull until there is no more slack, but do not over-tighten. I suggest doing this after sewing on every two signatures.

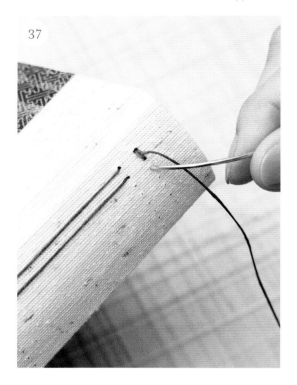

## Odd-Numbered Signature

37. Let's add a new signature. With the front cover positioned towards you, sew in through station 6 of the cover, next to the newly sewn signature. Pick up a new signature and place it in front of the previous one, checking that the holes are aligned between the signatures. Sew in through station 6 of the new signature. Pull the thread and bring the signature and cover to touch.

38. Sew out through station 5 of the signature, then through station 5 of the cover to the outside.

39. Sew in through station 4 of the cover, then through station 4 of the signature to the inside.

40. Sew out through station 3 of the signature, then through station 3 of the cover to the outside.

41. Sew in through station 2 of the cover, then through station 2 of the signature to the inside.

42. Sew out through station 1 of the signature, then through station 1 of the cover to the outside.

43. Create a kettle stitch (page 23) with the stitch of the previous signature by sewing behind the stitch between the previous signatures to create a loop, then pull taut.

44. Repeat steps 30 through 35 for sewing on the 4th signature and all subsequent even-numbered signatures. Create a kettle stitch with the stitch of the previous signature on the outside spine and pull taut.

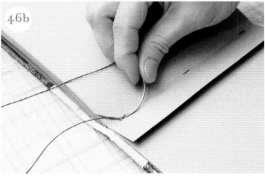

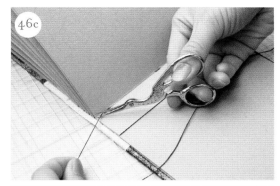

45. Repeat steps 37 through 42 for sewing on the 5th signature and all subsequent odd-numbered signatures. Create a kettle stitch (page 23) with the stitch of the previous signature on the outside spine and pull taut.

46. When the last signature is sewn on, pass your needle and working thread to the inside. Secure the sewing by tying a double half hitch knot (page 23). Cut the excess thread.

It's normal for the book to be a bit floppy until the pages are filled out. I suggest adding ribbon ties to keep the book closed. You can attach ribbons by following the instructions on page 176.

To mount photos into the album, I suggest using sticker photo corners, which are available at the arts and crafts store. Avoid using adhesive directly on the photo for preservation purposes.

# hardcover flat-back and round-back books

*timeless classics*

Featuring hard covers and spines that do an excellent job of protecting the pages, these book structures feel familiar and nostalgic. Books with flat and rounded spines are quite durable and open a path into more advanced bookbinding techniques.

## Sewn Boards Binding
### *Journal with Breakaway Spine*

- - - - - - - - - - - - - - - - - - - - - - - - - - - - - - - - - - - - - - - - - - - - - - - - - - - - - -

*The structure of Sewn Boards Binding is intriguing! The boards are not sewn with the text block per se but are cleverly slipped into the first and last signatures. The cloth spine "breaks away" from the text block when the book is opened.*

*This project uses the French Link Stitch to sew the text block. You will also learn a gluing technique called drumming, which uses minimal glue, reducing the risk of papers unexpectedly expanding and warping. With the exception of the signatures, accurate paper grain is not necessary to make a great Sewn Boards book. There are a lot of pieces in this project, but it's totally doable. Go slow and take it step by step!*

- - - - - - - - - - - - - - - - - - - - - - - - - - - - - - - - - - - - - - - - - - - - - - - - - - - - - -

**Difficulty:** ★ ★ ★

**New skills:** making a spine wrap, tipping in endpapers, drumming (gluing method)

- - - - - - - - - - - - - - - - - - - - - - - - - - - - - - - - - - - - - - - - - - - - - - - - - - - - - -

## materials

- 40 sheets of 8½ x 11 inch (21.6 x 27.9 cm) writing or sketch paper, 60–80lb (90–120gsm) text weight, grain short
- 2 sheets of 8½ x 11 inch (21.6 x 27.9 cm) endpaper, medium weight preferred, grain short (see page 16 for options)
- Waste sheets for gluing
- PVA glue
- 2 sheets of 8½ x 11 inch (21.6 x 27.9 cm) card stock paper, 80–100lb (216–270gsm) cover weight, grain short preferred
- Strip of stiff paper cut to 8½ inches (21.6 cm) in length and 2–3 inches (5–7.6 cm) in width
- Waxed linen thread, ²⁵/₃ gauge (thin)
- 2 sheets of 5½ x 8½ inch (14 x 21.6 cm) book board, 0.059–0.08 inch (1.5–2 mm) thick, grain long (preferred) or short
- 1 sheet of 8½ x 11 inch (21.6 x 27.9 cm) 60–80lb (90–120gsm) text weight paper, grain long
- 2 pieces of scrap book board larger than 5½ x 8½ inches (14 x 21.6 cm) with the long side clear taped
- 1 sheet of card stock paper, 8½ inches (21.6 cm) long and at least 2 inches (5 cm) wide, 80–100lb (216–270gsm) cover weight, grain long
- 1 strip of 3.5 x 11 inch (8.9 x 27.9 cm) book cloth
- 2 sheets of 6 x 10 inch (15.2 x 25.4 cm) decorative paper, medium to heavyweight, grain long (preferred) or short
- Moisture barrier sheets

## tools

- Bone folder
- Glue brush
- Pencil
- Metal ruler
- Awl
- Scissors
- Needle
- Cutting mat
- Utility knife
- Pressing equipment: book press, clamps or weights

Tip: The breakaway spine structure is perfect for making sleek-looking journals that lay fairly flat.

## Making the Text Block

1.    Start by folding five sheets of writing or sketch paper in half, with the short edges meeting each other. Crease the fold with the bone folder. Flip the folded papers vertically and crease the fold one more time. This is the first signature, which should measure 5½ x 8½ inches (14 x 21.6 cm). Make seven more signatures like this with the remaining sheets.

2a

2b

2. Let's attach the endpapers, which are found at the beginning and end of a book. One at a time, fold the two endpaper sheets in half with the smooth or patterned side on the inside. Crease the fold with the bone folder. Use a waste sheet with a straight edge to mask the first endpaper, leaving a narrow strip, about ⅛ inch (3 mm), at the fold. Use your glue brush to apply PVA glue to the exposed narrow strip. Attach the endpaper onto one of the signatures, lining up the folded edges without exceeding the signature. This method of attaching endpapers is called "tipping in." Press along the glued edge to adhere. Tip in the remaining endpaper onto another signature. Hold the signatures together with the endpapers on the front and back of the book.

3

3. One at a time, fold the two sheets of card stock paper in half and crease the folds with the bone folder. Place the card stock folios at the front and back of the signatures, on top of and underneath the endpapers. The text block is now ready for sewing. The card stock folios are treated as signatures and will be sewn with the original eight signatures, adding up to a total of ten signatures for this project. The endpapers will not be sewn.

4. Follow the instructions for the French Link Stitch (page 46), steps 3 through 21 for sewing the text block. Throughout those steps, you will be using the strip of stiff paper, ruler, pencil, awl, thread, scissors and needle. Once the text block is sewn, optionally trim the fore edge with the utility knife and metal ruler to create a smooth edge (instructions on page 25).

5. Measure and write down the width and length of the text block. Trim the two book boards to the same size as the text block. Sandwich the text block with the boards and ensure all of the edges are flush. Then slip the boards into the first and last card stock folios and align all the pieces on the spine edge. Holding the text block with both hands, push the boards into the fold of the card stock folio as you use your fingers to form the card stock over the board edge. Remove the boards to prepare for gluing.

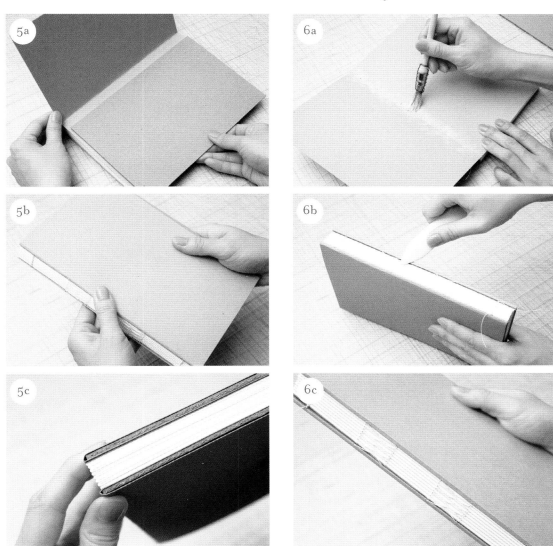

6. Let's attach the cover boards. Brush minimal glue in the gutter of the card stock folios, spanning about ½ inch (1.3 cm) on either side of the stitching. Attach the book board, checking for alignment at the head and tail. Hold the book with the spine down to align the cover with the spine. Use your fingers or the bone folder to mold the glued paper around the board edge. Repeat this step for the remaining book board. Tap the working book on the spine edge to align the signatures. Unlike typical hardcover books, the text block is flush with the cover boards.

Note: Gluing papers at the edges rather than the whole sheet is a gluing method called "drumming." Drumming introduces minimal moisture, which is intended to prevent the risk of paper warping. Use a tray to dip your glue brush into to control the amount of glue used.

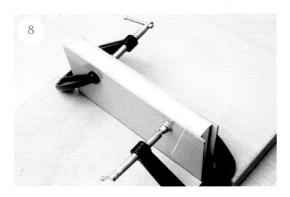

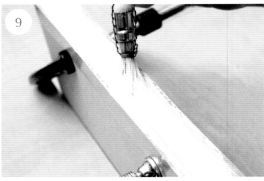

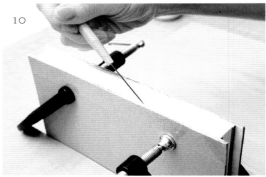

## Pressing and Gluing the Spine

When pressing the spine, aim to reduce the thickness of the spine slightly to be level with the fore edge as much as possible. It's important to not over-tighten, which can cause the signatures to fall out of alignment.

7.   Place the text block in between two scrap book boards, with their taped edges lined up with the spine. The taped edges will prevent the text block from sticking to the boards. Tap the text block and board sandwich on the desk to bring the signatures to alignment along the spine.

8.   Gluing the spine is easiest if the text block is pressed and propped up vertically with the spine facing up. Here are a few ways you can press the spine.

•   If you have a book press, slide the sandwiched text block into the press with ¼ inch (6 mm) of the spine edge extending beyond the edge of the press. Press the text block and lift the press to stand vertically.

•   Using C-clamps or spring clamps, press the sandwiched text block, making sure there is even pressure along the spine. Avoid pinching any part of the spine and over-tightening the clamps. Prop up the text block between two boxy weights to stand (image 8).

•   The text block can be pressed under weights as it lays horizontally. Have ¼ inch (6 mm) of the spine edge extend beyond the weights so that you can work on the spine. Use stable weights to prevent shifting.

9.   Cut the thread ends down to about ¼ inch (6 mm). Brush a generous layer of PVA glue along the length of the spine, but not so much that it pools and seeps in between the signatures. Using an awl or the tip of the brush handle, tuck the thread ends in between the signatures. Use the tip of the brush to stipple glue over the links or use your fingers to push glue into hard-to-reach areas. Cover all the gaps in the spine and let the glue dry to touch.

10.  Brush two to three more thin coats of glue, letting each coat dry before applying a new one. Let the glue dry completely in the press, at least 20 minutes.

Tip: Run the tip of the awl between the outer signatures and the pressing boards to remove glue for easier detaching later on.

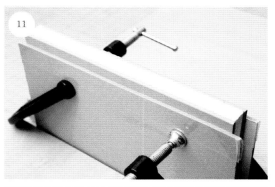

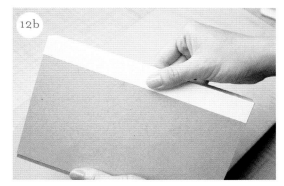

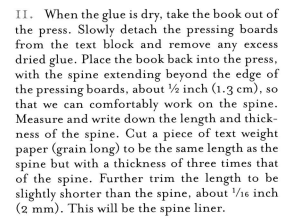

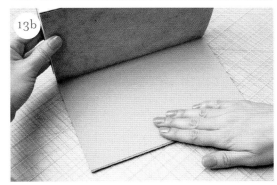

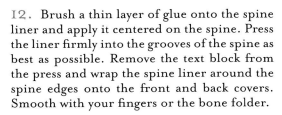

II. When the glue is dry, take the book out of the press. Slowly detach the pressing boards from the text block and remove any excess dried glue. Place the book back into the press, with the spine extending beyond the edge of the pressing boards, about ½ inch (1.3 cm), so that we can comfortably work on the spine. Measure and write down the length and thickness of the spine. Cut a piece of text weight paper (grain long) to be the same length as the spine but with a thickness of three times that of the spine. Further trim the length to be slightly shorter than the spine, about ¹⁄₁₆ inch (2 mm). This will be the spine liner.

I2. Brush a thin layer of glue onto the spine liner and apply it centered on the spine. Press the liner firmly into the grooves of the spine as best as possible. Remove the text block from the press and wrap the spine liner around the spine edges onto the front and back covers. Smooth with your fingers or the bone folder.

I3. Let's further secure the cover boards. Starting with the front cover, gently lift the outer card stock leaf and brush minimal glue onto the head, tail and fore edges of the board, about ¾ inch (1.9 cm) from the edges. Press on the card stock from the spine moving outward to adhere. Repeat for all sides of the front and back cover boards.

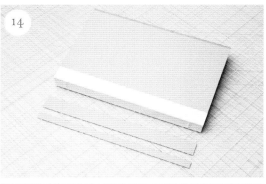

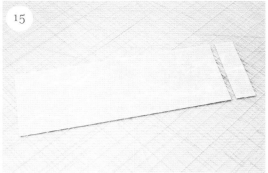

## Making the Spine Wrap

The spine wrap is a piece of book cloth stiffened with card stock paper. The cloth material gives it the flexibility to break away from the book when opened. It also adds structure and protection for the spine. You may want to choose a card stock color that matches the book cloth color, since you'll be able to see some of it when the book is open.

14. Cut a strip of card stock paper that is the same length as the spine but slightly less wide (about $1/16$ inch [2 mm]). My spine width is $13/16$ inch (2.1 cm), so I cut a spine strip that is ¾ inch (1.9 cm) wide. This will be the spine stiffener. Cut one more strip that is the same length as the spine and ⅜ inch (1 cm) wide. This thinner strip will be used later as a mask for attaching the spine wrap.

15. Prepare the book cloth by checking that the edges are straight and square. Trim the edges if needed. Trim off a 1-inch (2.5 cm) piece from the length and set aside to use later. On the paper side of the book cloth, mark the midway point on the short edges with a pencil. Draw a light line down the middle, connecting the points. Mark midpoints on the head and tail of the spine stiffener as well.

16. Working on a waste sheet, brush a thin layer of glue onto the blank side of the spine stiffener, and apply it onto the center of the book cloth, aligning the pencil lines. Rub it on with the bone folder.

17. Brush a thin layer of glue onto the tab at the head, fold the tab over the spine stiffener, then press it flat. While the glue is wet, pull the corners down so the top edge is ever so slightly turned downwards on either side of the spine stiffener. This will prevent cloth corners from sticking beyond the edges of the book. Repeat this gluing method for the book cloth tab at the tail.

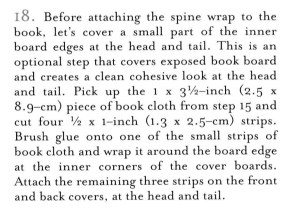

18. Before attaching the spine wrap to the book, let's cover a small part of the inner board edges at the head and tail. This is an optional step that covers exposed book board and creates a clean cohesive look at the head and tail. Pick up the 1 x 3½-inch (2.5 x 8.9-cm) piece of book cloth from step 15 and cut four ½ x 1-inch (1.3 x 2.5-cm) strips. Brush glue onto one of the small strips of book cloth and wrap it around the board edge at the inner corners of the cover boards. Attach the remaining three strips on the front and back covers, at the head and tail.

19. The book is ready for the spine wrap to be attached. With the inside spine wrap facing up, place the ⅜-inch (1-cm)-wide strip of card stock paper on one side of the spine stiffener. This space will allow for the spine to break away from the text block. Brush a thin layer of glue onto the book cloth beyond the mask. Stipple glue onto the top and bottom tabs with the tips of the bristles. Place the mask on the other side of the spine stiffener and brush glue onto the remaining book cloth side. Be sure to leave the ⅜ inch (1 cm) gap dry.

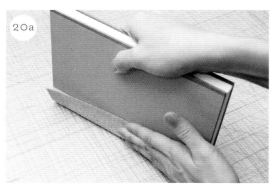

20. Remove the mask and place the text block spine onto the spine stiffener, lining up all the edges. Holding the book down to anchor the spine wrap, lift up one side of the spine wrap and press it against the text block. Attach the other side, making sure the spine wrap is snug against the text block. Holding the spine with your hand, push the spine wrap towards the fore edge.

## Covering the Boards

The decorative paper helps seal the edges of the book cloth and encase the sheets of the cover boards. Using a heavier weight decorative paper helps hide any bumps and ridges. Optionally, you can drum on a "filler" paper between the cloth and the fore edge to even out the layers on the cover.

21. Prepare the sheets of decorative paper. Lay the book flat with the spine on the left. Place the ⅜-inch (1-cm) card stock mask along the spine edge to use as a spacer. Using a pencil or pen that will show up on the fabric, mark dots at the head and tail on the book cloth next to the spacer. Make marks on both the front and back covers. This is the meeting point where the decorative paper will overlap the book cloth.

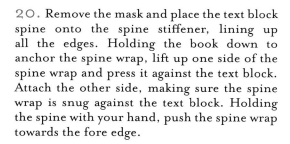

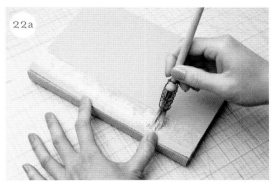

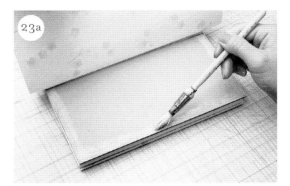

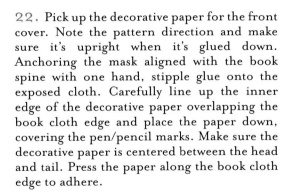

22. Pick up the decorative paper for the front cover. Note the pattern direction and make sure it's upright when it's glued down. Anchoring the mask aligned with the book spine with one hand, stipple glue onto the exposed cloth. Carefully line up the inner edge of the decorative paper overlapping the book cloth edge and place the paper down, covering the pen/pencil marks. Make sure the decorative paper is centered between the head and tail. Press the paper along the book cloth edge to adhere.

23. Drum on the decorative paper by keeping it lifted as you brush minimal glue onto the head, tail and fore edges of the board, ½ to ¾ inch (1.3 to 1.9 cm) from the edges. Gently lay the paper down towards the fore edge. Press the paper thoroughly with your palms to adhere and gently rub on the decorative paper using the length of the bone folder moving from the center outward.

24. Cut the two corners of the decorative paper at the fore edge at a 45-degree angle, leaving about ⅛ inch (3 mm) of excess at the board corner. This tiny space is important for the next step of neatly wrapping the cover material around the book board, also known as turn-ins. The excess space should be slightly wider than the thickness of the board.

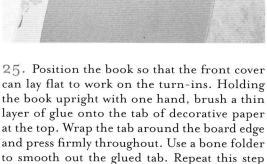

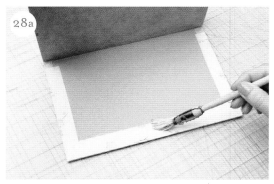

25. Position the book so that the front cover can lay flat to work on the turn-ins. Holding the book upright with one hand, brush a thin layer of glue onto the tab of decorative paper at the top. Wrap the tab around the board edge and press firmly throughout. Use a bone folder to smooth out the glued tab. Repeat this step for the tab on the opposite side.

26. Brush glue on the remaining tab at the fore edge. Use the bone folder to tuck in and press the corner bits flat. Wrap the tab over the book board's edge. Rub on and smooth with the bone folder.

27. Repeat steps 22 to 26 to attach decorative paper onto the back cover.

28. Let's complete the book by attaching the endpapers. With one cover open towards you, hold the book upright along the fore edge with your non-dominant hand. Brush minimal glue on the inner cover board at the head, tail, and fore edges, ½ to ¾ inch (1.3 to 1.9 cm) from the edges. Lay down the endpaper slowly, pressing from the spine moving outward. The endpaper should be lined up to the edges of the cover. Press on the endpaper with your hands, then smooth over with the long edge of the bone folder. Repeat this step for the remaining endpaper.

29. Place moisture barrier sheets at the inner covers to protect the text block from moisture seeping from the glue. Let the book lay flat to dry. You can lightly press the book with a weight on top to further flatten the book. Let the book dry overnight before opening it again.

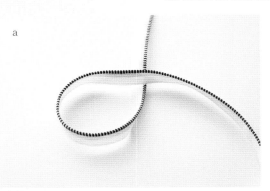

## Endbands and Bookmarks to Complete the Look

I love adding ribbon bookmarks and endbands to hardcover books. For the bookmark, choose a quality ribbon that is ¼ to ⅜ inch (6 to 10 mm) in width, proportional to the size of the text block. The bookmark is attached with glue after the spine is lined and before the endbands are installed.

Endbands fill in the space at the head and tail of the spine in between the case and the text block. They are both aesthetic and structural, adding support to the text block. Endbands are traditionally sewn into the text block with silk threads. You can buy pre-made endbands by the yard from bookbinding supply shops (image A) or make your own out of fabric to match the book cloth.

To make endbands, you will need fabric, cotton twine, and PVA glue. Cut a 1-inch (2.5-cm) strip of fabric slightly wider than the spine width. Brush glue onto the wrong side of the fabric, and lay the cotton twine across, on the top one-third of the strip.

Fold the short side over the twine and press to adhere. Push the twine into the fold with the edge of the bone folder or ruler to form the piping (image B). Trim the width to match the text block thickness. Attach them onto the head and tail of the text block with PVA glue above the kettle stitch (image C).

Endbands and bookmarks are part of all the following hardcover book projects from page 138–167.

# Case Binding
## *Minimal Journal*

- - - - - - - - - - - - - - - - - - - - - - - - - - - - - - - - - - - - - - - - - - - - - - - - - - -

*Case binding is the quintessential hardcover book structure and one of my favorites to make. It's typically the next step for beginner bookbinders to make books with hard backs. The text block and hardcover case are built separately, then assembled at the end. Use this binding to make any kind of journal or sketchbook with light- to medium-weight paper. This project will be covered fully with book cloth and include matching endbands and a ribbon bookmark.*

- - - - - - - - - - - - - - - - - - - - - - - - - - - - - - - - - - - - - - - - - - - - - - - - - - -

### Difficulty: ★ ★ ★

**New skills:** lining the spine, constructing a hardcover case, adding a bookmark and endbands, casing in, pressing the completed book, forming hinges/joints

- - - - - - - - - - - - - - - - - - - - - - - - - - - - - - - - - - - - - - - - - - - - - - - - - - -

## materials

- 40 sheets of 8½ x 11 inch (21.6 x 27.9 cm) writing or sketch paper, 60–80lb (90–120gsm) text weight, grain short
- Strip of stiff paper cut to 8½ inches (21.6 cm) in length and 2–3 inches (5–7.6 cm) in width
- Waxed linen thread, ²⁵/₃ gauge (thin)
- 2 sheets of 8½ x 11 inch (21.6 x 27.9 cm) endpapers, medium weight preferred, grain short (see page 16 for options)
- Waste sheets for gluing
- PVA glue
- 2 pieces of scrap book board larger than 5½ x 8½ inches (14 x 21.6 cm) with long side clear taped
- Mull, cut to 8½ inches (21.6 cm) long and 3 inches (7.6 cm) wide
- Japanese tissue paper (optional), cut to 8½ inches (21.6 cm) long and 3 inches (7.6 cm) wide
- Ribbon for bookmark, ¼–⅜ inch (6–10 mm) wide
- Endbands (see page 137 for options)
- 1 sheet of book board, at least 8¾ x 12 inches (22.2 x 30.5 cm), 0.08-inch (2 mm), short grain
- 1 sheet of 10½ x 14 inch (26.7 x 35.6 cm) book cloth
- Moisture barrier sheets

## tools

- Bone folder
- Metal ruler
- Pencil
- Awl
- Scissors
- Needle
- Glue brush
- Pressing equipment: book press, clamps or weights
- Cutting mat
- Utility knife
- Artist tape or washi tape
- ⅜-inch (1 cm) spacer
- ¾-inch (1.9 cm) spacer
- Rotary cutter
- 2 hinge rods or double-pointed knitting needles size 0–2 (2–2.75 mm), at least 8 inches (20.3 cm) long
- Lighter for sealing the ribbon

## Making the Text Block

1. Start by folding four sheets of writing or sketch paper in half, with the short edges meeting each other. Crease the fold with the bone folder. Flip the folded papers vertically and crease the fold one more time. This is the first signature, which should measure 5½ x 8½ inches (14 x 21.6 cm). Make nine more signatures like this.

2. Follow the instructions for the French Link Stitch (page 46), steps 3 through 21 for sewing the text block. Throughout those steps, you will be using the strip of stiff paper, ruler, pencil, awl, thread, scissors and needle.

3a

3b

## Pressing and Lining the Spine

When pressing the text block to prepare the spine for gluing, aim to reduce the thickness of the spine slightly and to keep it level with the fore edge as much as possible. It's important to not over-tighten, which can cause the signatures to fall out of alignment along the spine. Gluing and lining the spine with supportive materials will ensure that the book will be strong and flexible to withstand use.

3. Fold the two endpaper sheets in half one at a time with the smooth or patterned side on the inside and crease the fold with the bone folder. Use a waste sheet with a straight edge to mask the first endpaper, leaving a narrow strip, about ⅛ inch (3 mm), at the fold. Use your glue brush to apply PVA glue to the exposed narrow strip. Attach the endpaper onto one side of the text block, lining up the folded edges without exceeding the signature. This method of attaching endpapers is called "tipping in." Press along the glued edge to adhere. Tip in the remaining endpaper onto the other side of the text block.

Note: When pressing the text block, aim to align the signatures at the head and tail as best as possible for smooth and level edges.

4. Place the text block in between two scrap book boards, with the taped edges lined up with the spine. The taped edges will prevent the text block from sticking to the boards. Tap the text block and board sandwich on the desk to bring the signatures to alignment along the spine.

5. Gluing the spine is easiest if the text block is pressed and propped up vertically with the spine facing up. Apply consistent medium pressing force on the signature folds along the spine. Here are a few ways you can press the spine.

• If you have a book press, slide the sandwiched text block into the press with ¼ inch (6 mm) of the spine edge extending beyond the edge of the press. Press the text block and lift the press to stand vertically.

• Using spring clamps or C-clamps, press the sandwiched text block, making sure there is even pressure along the spine. Avoid pinching any part of the spine and over-tightening the clamps. Prop up the text block between two boxy weights to stand.

• The text block can be pressed under weights as it lays horizontally. Place the sandwiched text block in between two boxy weights, such as heavy books. Have ¼ inch (6 mm) of the spine edge extend beyond the weights so that you can work on the spine. Use stable weights to prevent shifting.

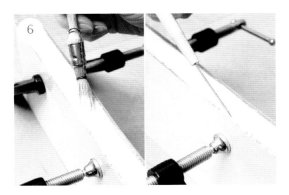

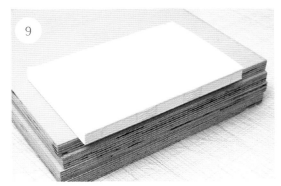

6. Cut the thread ends down to about a ¼ inch (6 mm). Brush a generous layer of PVA glue along the length of the spine, but not so much that it pools and seeps in between the signatures. Using an awl or the tip of the brush handle, tuck the thread ends in between the signatures. Use the tip of the brush to stipple glue over the links or use your fingers to push glue into hard-to-reach areas. Cover all of the gaps in the spine and let the glue dry to touch.

Tip: Run the tip of the awl between the outer signatures and the pressing boards to remove glue for easier detaching later.

7. Brush two to three more thin coats of glue, letting each coat dry before applying a new one. Let the glue dry completely in the press, at least 20 minutes.

8. Take the book out of the press. Slowly detach the pressing boards from the text block and remove any excess dried glue. Optionally, trim the fore edge with the utility knife and metal ruler (instructions on page 25).

9. Let's line the spine with strengthening and decorative materials. Place the book back into the press with the spine extending beyond the edge of the pressing boards, about ½ inch (1.3 cm).

Note: I prefer when the text block is propped upright, but you can work on the spine on flat, lifted platforms as it lays horizontally.

10. Confirm that the strip of mull is the same length as the spine. Brush on a thin layer of glue along the length of the spine. Center the mull onto the spine and lay it on. Press firmly with your fingers to adhere and rub on with the bone folder. It's important for the mull to be attached fully, forming over all the little bumps on the spine, so that the mull can do its job of supporting spine movement.

Tip: If you prefer extra spine support, add another layer of thin, Japanese tissue paper.

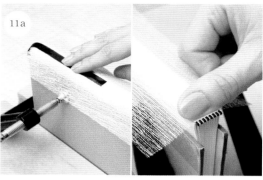

II. Working on a waste sheet, brush glue onto 3 to 4 inches (7.6 to 10.2 cm) of one end of the ribbon. Center the ribbon onto the spine and attach it at the head side. Press and hold the ribbon to adhere. Brush glue onto one endband, avoiding the piping, and stipple glue onto the text block and ribbon, being careful not to get glue on the part of the ribbon that will be visible beyond the text block. Attach the endband onto the text block. Press and hold to adhere. Glue on the remaining endband. Carefully remove the text block from the press. Measure out the ribbon to be at least 3 inches (7.6 cm) longer than the length of the book and trim it with scissors. Slip the ribbon bookmark into the middle of the text block, leaving some slack at the top so the adhesive is not disturbed. Confirm that all of the spine linings are adhered and set the text block aside to dry.

## Making the Hardcover Case

It's best practice to measure and cut the boards for the hardcover case after the text block is complete. With each project, the text block results can vary, so it's important that the hardcover case is tailored to the text block for the best fit.

12. Let's start by making the front and back covers. Measure and write down the width and length of the text block. The cover boards will be the same width as the text block, but the length of the spine will be an additional ¼ inch (6 mm). The extra spacing creates a cover overhang of ⅛ inch (3 mm) at the head and tail. Cut two pieces of book board, with the grain running parallel to the spine. Hold the boards against the text block to confirm that the width is the same, and the length extends beyond the text block by ⅛ inch (3 mm) at the head and tail.

Note: Aim for the width of the spine board to be level with the thickness of the fore edge. When determining the spine width for a flat-back book, I've found that the thickness of the text block plus both boards is often slightly too wide, so I usually reduce it to the thickness of the text block plus one board.

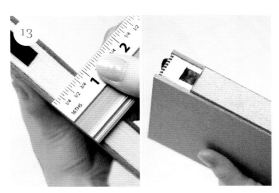

13. To measure the width of the spine board, keep holding the boards on either side of the text block and compress with one hand. Measure and write down the thickness of the text block plus one cover board. Cut a piece of spine board that is the same length as the cover boards, and the width that you just wrote down with the grain running lengthwise along the spine.

## Test Fitting the Hardcover Case

14. This is one way to check that the boards are the right size before committing to covering the boards. To test the fit of the case, use two pieces of artist or washi tape, about 5 inches (12.7 cm), and place them horizontally across the spine board. Flip the spine over and place a ⅜-inch (1-cm) spacer on one side, against the spine board. Then place a cover board against the spacer, checking for alignment at the head and tail. Move the spacer to the other side of the spine board and place the remaining cover board. Remove the spacer and wrap the boards around the text block. Push the text block firmly into the inner spine and center it between the head and tail, pulling the covers outward to maximize the hinge gap. The hinge gap may seem roomy now, but once the cover material is applied, the hinge will be stabilized.

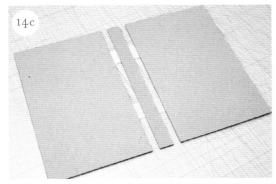

Check that there is an even overhang trim, about ⅛ inch (3 mm) around the head, tail and fore edge. The fore edge is likely to be too long. With a pencil, mark where the text block fore edge ends on the cover boards. Measure and mark ⅛ inch (3 mm) past this mark to indicate the cover overhang. Make the same marks on the opposite cover and, with your ruler and utility knife, trim both boards to size. Trim any other part of the case to your liking and test fit the case after each adjustment. Note that the book cloth will add some bulk to all sides of the cover.

Note: Experiment with the width of the hinge gap to find your preference. As a general rule, thicker boards and cover materials will require a wider gap. A common hinge gap space for small- to medium-sized case bound books is ¼ inch (6 mm). I've found that ⅜ inch (1 cm) also works well, as it allows covers to open more loosely, resulting in a book that lies flatter when opened.

15. Once you're happy with the fit, measure and mark the midway point on a short edge of the book cloth and make the same mark on the opposite side. Draw a horizontal line across by connecting the points.

16. Measure and mark the midway point on a long edge of the book cloth and make the same mark on the opposite side. Draw a vertical midline by connecting the points. These lines will be helpful for centering and squaring the boards.

17. Brush a thin layer of glue onto the spine board. Attach it squarely onto the center of the book cloth, using the midlines as guides.

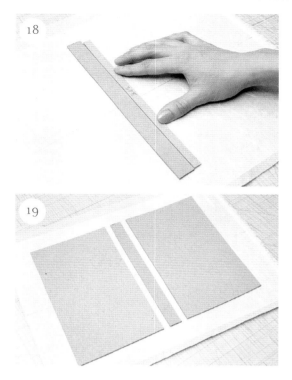

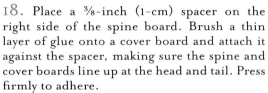

18. Place a ⅜-inch (1-cm) spacer on the right side of the spine board. Brush a thin layer of glue onto a cover board and attach it against the spacer, making sure the spine and cover boards line up at the head and tail. Press firmly to adhere.

19. Repeat step 18 for the left side of the spine board.

20. Flip the cover over and rub on the book cloth with the long edge of the bone folder with medium pressure. Smooth from the center moving outward. Score the hinges by digging the tip of the bone folder into the hinge gaps pressing along the edges of the boards. This will help form a groove at the hinge and allow for more movement when opening the cover.

21. Flip the cover over. Trim each edge of the book cloth with a ¾-inch (1.9-cm) spacer and rotary cutter. If you don't have a spacer, measure and mark ¾ inch (1.9 cm) from each edge of the cover board. Cut each corner of the decorative paper at a 45-degree angle, leaving about ⅛ inch (3 mm) of excess. This tiny space should be slightly wider than the thickness of the board, and is important for neat turn-ins.

22. Starting at the top edge of the cover, brush a thin layer of glue onto the tab of book cloth. Wrap the tab around the board and press firmly throughout. Smooth out the glued tab with a bone folder. Press the book cloth into the hinge gap with the bone folder. Repeat for the tab on the opposite side.

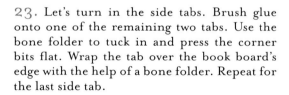

23. Let's turn in the side tabs. Brush glue onto one of the remaining two tabs. Use the bone folder to tuck in and press the corner bits flat. Wrap the tab over the book board's edge with the help of a bone folder. Repeat for the last side tab.

The case is complete! Lay the cover flat to dry, at least 20 minutes. You can also lightly press it under weights to flatten it while it dries. It is normal if the covers bow out slightly when they're dry. Gluing the endpapers to the inner covers will "pull" the cover inward to straighten out. The goal is to find a balance between the pulling forces of different materials glued onto the outer and inner covers.

## Casing in the Text Block

The text block is cased in by gluing each endpaper onto the inner covers one at a time. It can be difficult to get everything aligned in the beginning, so don't be discouraged! Try to move decisively, especially since PVA glue sets quickly. Have dry waste sheets and moisture barrier sheets ready as each endpaper is glued. I encourage you to read through this section before attempting it.

> Note: The spine will not be glued as the spacing in between the text block and case allows the book to open and close.

24. Test fit the case over the text block. Visually note the cover overhang at the fore edge, which will be helpful for the next step. To set up, position the book with the fore edge facing you. Open the cover and prop it up at an angle on an object. Center the text block on the back cover between the head and tail. Slip a waste sheet under the top endpaper leaf.

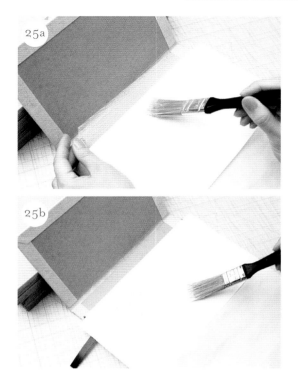

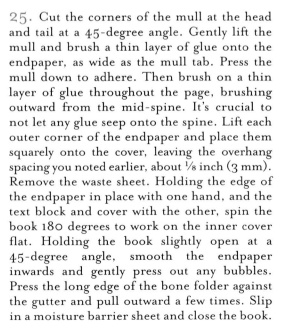

25. Cut the corners of the mull at the head and tail at a 45-degree angle. Gently lift the mull and brush a thin layer of glue onto the endpaper, as wide as the mull tab. Press the mull down to adhere. Then brush on a thin layer of glue throughout the page, brushing outward from the mid-spine. It's crucial to not let any glue seep onto the spine. Lift each outer corner of the endpaper and place them squarely onto the cover, leaving the overhang spacing you noted earlier, about ⅛ inch (3 mm). Remove the waste sheet. Holding the edge of the endpaper in place with one hand, and the text block and cover with the other, spin the book 180 degrees to work on the inner cover flat. Holding the book slightly open at a 45-degree angle, smooth the endpaper inwards and gently press out any bubbles. Press the long edge of the bone folder against the gutter and pull outward a few times. Slip in a moisture barrier sheet and close the book.

Note: During this process, try your best to ensure the text block is fitted against the spine board as much as possible. This will help the hinges function properly so that the book can open fully.

26. Flip the book over to glue the other side. Position the book with the spine on the left side. If you're left-handed, position the book with the spine on the right side. Open the remaining cover. Slip a dry waste sheet under the top endpaper leaf. Cut the corners of the mull at the head and tail at a 45-degree angle. Glue down the mull first, then brush glue throughout the endpaper, brushing from the mid-spine moving outward. Lift the endpaper leaf with one hand and lift the cover with the other hand. Attach the fore edge of the endpaper squarely onto the cover as best you can, leaving the overhang spacing you noted, about ⅛ inch (3 mm). Don't adhere the whole sheet. Holding the cover and endpaper with one hand, and the book with the other hand, flip the book over to work on the inner cover flat. Hold the book slightly open at a 45-degree angle with one hand, pressing the spine down into the cover. Adjust the endpaper alignment by gently lifting the glued sheet and re-positioning if the glue is still wet, aiming for an even cover overhang on all three edges. Keep the text block pressed into the spine as you smooth down the endpaper inwards towards the gutter. Press the long edge of the bone folder along the gutter and pull outward a few times. Slip in a moisture barrier sheet and close the book. Alternatively, you can use the method described in step 25 if you prefer.

Note: If your endpapers are misaligned or wrinkled when you're casing in your first books, that's okay! This process will take some practice. You can try using heavier weight papers. They generally don't expand as much when moisture is introduced, making them easier to work with as endpapers.

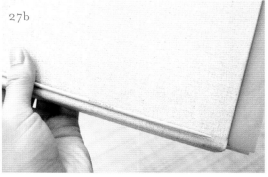

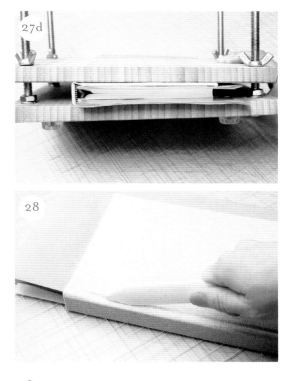

27. Nice, you just cased in a book! Use the tip of the bone folder to score the hinges on the book cloth. For more pronounced grooves, place hinge rods or double-pointed knitting needles into the hinge gap. With the hinge rods and moisture barrier sheets in place, press the book horizontally for at least 8 hours (or overnight) to dry. It's normal to need to re-position the hinge rods as you put the book in the press. You can press the book with a book press or between pressing boards with weights on top. Do not over-tighten the press to minimize the risk of glue seeping into the hinges and spine. The book should be compressed just enough until every component is flat and there is no visible spacing between the covers, and above and below the book.

Note: Your location, the time of year, and weather conditions can affect the drying time! The more humid and rainier your climate is, the longer it will take for glue to dry.

28. Pulling the book out of the press is the highlight of case binding! Carefully remove the moisture barrier sheets as they may be stuck on from seeping glue. Before opening the book, check that the covers, spine and text block lay flat and square. The book needs to be opened methodically to warm up the spine. Open the book all the way at the middle, then the first third of the book and finally the last third of the book. Flip through the pages to test for smooth spine movement. Open the inner covers to check the endpapers. If an additional trim is needed, cut the ribbon bookmark to the desired length, then seal the ribbon edge with a lighter.

Note: Heavier weight papers, such as mixed media or watercolor paper, are not suitable for flat-back and round-back books due to the stiffness of the paper, which creates a lack of drape of the pages.

# Three Piece Bradel Binding
## *Color-Block Journal*

*This is a fun variation of case binding where the spine and covers can be made with different colors or materials. It's known for the separate spine piece that is affixed to the inner covers, which helps the book open more readily. Bradel binding was developed in Germany as a versatile book structure.*

*In this project, I use book cloth in two contrasting colors for the covers. Using thin book cloth will be important for minimizing bulk at the hinge. Creating the text block and casing it into the hardcover is the same process as case binding.*

**Difficulty:** ★ ★ ★

**New skills:** variation on constructing a hardcover case

## materials

- 40 sheets of 8½ x 11 inch (21.6 x 27.9 cm) writing or sketch paper, 60–80lb (90–120gsm) text weight, grain short
- Strip of stiff paper cut to 8½ inches (21.6 cm) in length and 2–3 inches (5–7.6 cm) in width
- Waxed linen thread, ²⁵/₃ gauge (thin)
- 2 sheets of 8½ x 11 inch (21.6 x 27.9 cm) endpapers, medium weight preferred, grain short (see page 16 for options)
- Waste sheets for gluing
- PVA glue
- 2 pieces of scrap book board larger than 5½ x 8½ inches (14 x 21.6 cm) with long side clear taped
- Mull, cut to 8½ inches (21.6 cm) long and 3 inches (7.6 cm) wide
- Japanese tissue paper (optional), cut to 8½ inches (21.6 cm) long and 3 inches (7.6 cm) wide
- Ribbon for bookmark, ¼–⅜ inch (6–10 mm) wide
- Endbands (see page 137 for options)
- 1 sheet of book board, at least 8¾ x 12 inches (22.2 x 30.5 cm), 0.08 inch (2 mm), short grain
- 1 sheet of 11 x 15 inch (27.9 x 38 cm) book cloth for the covers
- 1 sheet of 3½ x 11 inch (8.9 x 27.9 cm) book cloth for the spine, different color
- Moisture barrier sheets

## tools

- Bone folder
- Ruler
- Pencil
- Awl
- Scissors
- Needle
- Glue brush
- Pressing equipment: book press, clamps or weights
- Cutting mat
- Utility knife
- Artist or washi tape
- ⅜-inch (1-cm) spacer
- ¾-inch (1.9-cm) spacer
- Spring divider (optional)
- Rotary cutter
- 2 hinge rods or double-pointed knitting needles size 0–2 (2–2.75 mm), at least 8 inches (20.3 cm) long

To make the text block and prepare the cover boards, follow steps 1 through 14 in Case Binding (page 139). Then return to this project to assemble the hardcover case.

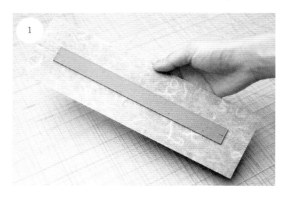

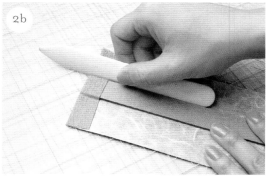

## Assembling the Hardcover Case

The three pieces of the case are made separately, and then assembled together. The spine piece has an expanding effect when attached onto the inner covers.

I.  Let's cover the boards with book cloth. Check that the book cloth pieces have straight and square edges. Pick up the spine book cloth and draw a midline lengthwise on the paper side. Mark the midpoints on the head and tail of the spine board as well. Glue the spine board onto the book cloth, aligning the midpoints and centering between the head and tail. Trim the left and right sides to measure 1¼ inches (3.2 cm) wide. Using a ¾-inch (1.9-cm) spacer, trim the book cloth at the head and tail.

2.  Brush a thin layer of glue onto the tab at the head and fold over the spine board. Press firmly to adhere. While the glue is wet, pull the corners down so the top edge is ever so slightly turned downwards on either side of the spine board. This will prevent cloth corners from sticking beyond the edges of the book. Use the edge of the bone folder to push the cloth into the board edge. Repeat this gluing for the book cloth tab at the tail. Flip the spine piece over and score the hinge by pressing the tip of the bone folder against the spine board edge.

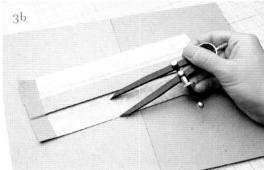

3. Place a ⅜-inch (1-cm) spacer on the right side of the spine board and draw a line on the book cloth to indicate the hinge gap. Repeat for the left side of the spine board. This line will also mark the placement of the covers. Measure the distance between the pencil line and the edge of the book cloth, about ⅞ inch (2.2 cm). Mark that measurement on both cover boards from the inner edge, at the head and tail. Draw a vertical line and connect the points. You can use a spring divider to quickly transfer the measurement from the book cloth to the cover boards.

Note: A spring divider is not necessary, but it can be a handy addition to your toolbox to help you accurately mark repeated measurements. Simply make pinhole marks into the board. My spring divider is 4 inches (10 cm) long.

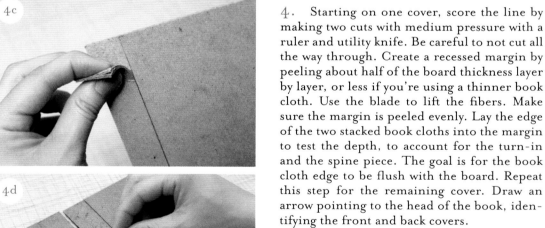

4. Starting on one cover, score the line by making two cuts with medium pressure with a ruler and utility knife. Be careful to not cut all the way through. Create a recessed margin by peeling about half of the board thickness layer by layer, or less if you're using a thinner book cloth. Use the blade to lift the fibers. Make sure the margin is peeled evenly. Lay the edge of the two stacked book cloths into the margin to test the depth, to account for the turn-in and the spine piece. The goal is for the book cloth edge to be flush with the board. Repeat this step for the remaining cover. Draw an arrow pointing to the head of the book, identifying the front and back covers.

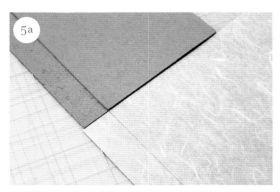

**Note:** Another way to build the covers with a recessed margin is to glue two thin boards together. The top board is narrower to create a recessed space for the spine piece.

5. Covering the boards is different from other bindings, as the recessed part of the board needs to be considered for the turn-ins. Prepare by checking that the large piece of book cloth has straight and square edges. Position the cloth with the long edge on top. Measure the width of the recessed space on the inner covers and add a tiny space for the thickness of the board. Mark the measurement on the top and bottom edges of the book cloth, from the left side. Draw a vertical line by connecting the points. Brush a thin layer of glue on the front side of the cover board. Position the inner cover edge on the pencil line, centered between the top and bottom edges, and press to adhere. Using the ¾-inch (1.9-cm) spacer, trim the book cloth at the head, tail and fore edges with a rotary cutter.

**Note:** Feel free to use decorative paper for the cover boards to add a different material, similar to quarter binding (page 110). This would also minimize some bulk at the hinges.

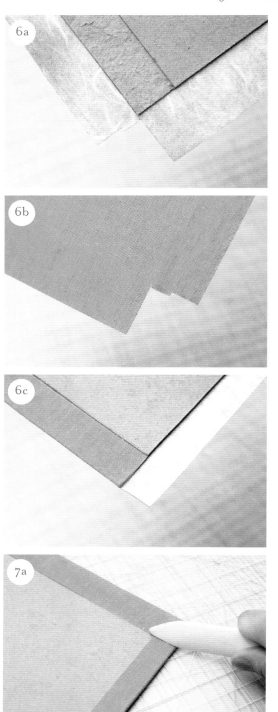

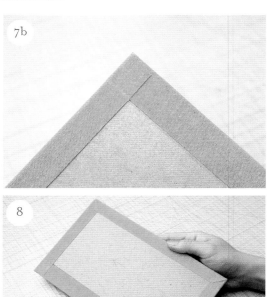

6.   Let's turn in the spine edge first. Cut the inner corners at a 90-degree angle with a small tab as shown. Test for the amount of bulk on the margin by folding over the spine tab and the bottom tab. Remember that we will also be attaching the spine piece on top. You can peel off some more board material to reduce bulk without compromising the strength of the board. Brush a thin layer of glue throughout the tab at the spine edge. Wrap the tab over the board and press firmly to adhere. Using the bone folder, tuck in the small tabs at the head and tail and rub on the glued tab.

7.   Trim the fore edge corners at a 45-degree angle, leaving a tiny space at the corner for the turn-ins. Trim the inner corners at a slight angle to prevent the cloth from sticking out beyond the board. Brush a thin layer of glue onto the tab at the head. Wrap the tab over the board's edge and press firmly. Rub on with the bone folder and press firmly into the recessed margin. Repeat for the opposite side.

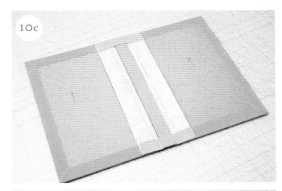

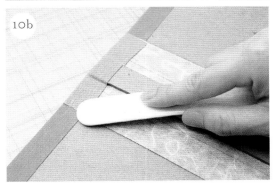

8.    Use the bone folder to tuck in and press the corner bits flat. Brush glue onto the remaining fore edge tab and wrap it over the book board's edge. Press firmly throughout and rub with a bone folder.

9.    Repeat steps 5 to 8 to apply the book cloth onto the remaining cover.

10.    Let's assemble the hardcover case. Place the covers and spine in order from left to right, with the recessed margins next to the spine. Brush or stipple glue onto the inner margin of the front cover, and a little bit of glue on the front side of the spine piece. Press the spine piece onto the cover, with the edge of the cloth meeting the score line on the cover. Glue the other side of the spine piece onto the back cover margin as well. Press and flatten the spine piece into the recessed margins as much as possible with the bone folder. Make sure the spine piece is adhered well to the covers. Lightly press the hardcover case with weights on top and set them aside to dry for at least a half hour.

To case in the text block and complete the book, follow steps 24 through 28 in Case Binding (page 139).

## Rounded Spine Book
*Thick Journal*

- - - - - - - - - - - - - - - - - - - - - - - - - - - - - - - - - - - - - - - - - - - - - - - -

*Rounded spine books bring me an unexplainable deep joy. It was exhilarating when I made my first rounded spine book. If you're looking to make a book with over 100 pages, you may need to consider this technique. The main reason for rounding is to reduce swell (page 181) and minimize stress on the book spine. Rounded spines are also beautiful! You can purposefully increase spine swell to achieve a rounded spine design.*

*This project closely follows the case binding method I shared earlier. Rounding the spine is not difficult but it will take some practice with the hammer. I recommend trying this project after you're more comfortable with case binding for flat-back books.*

- - - - - - - - - - - - - - - - - - - - - - - - - - - - - - - - - - - - - - - - - - - - - - - -

**Difficulty:** ★ ★ ★

**New skills:** rounding a text block, measuring a hardcover case for a rounded spine book

- - - - - - - - - - - - - - - - - - - - - - - - - - - - - - - - - - - - - - - - - - - - - - - -

## materials

- 52 sheets of 8½ x 11 inch (21.6 x 27.9 cm) writing or sketch paper, 60–80lb (90–120gsm) text weight, grain short
- Strip of stiff paper cut to 8½ inches (21.6 cm) in length and 2–3 inches (5–7.6 cm) in width
- Waxed linen thread, ²⁵/₃ gauge (thin)
- 2 sheets of 8½ x 11 inch (21.6 x 27.9 cm) endpapers, medium weight, grain short (see page 16 for options)
- Waste sheets for gluing
- PVA glue
- 2 pieces of scrap book board larger than 5½ x 8½ inches (14 x 21.6 cm) with long side clear taped
- Scrap paper strip for measuring the spine thickness
- Mull, cut to 8½ inches (21.6 cm) long and 3 inches (7.6 cm) wide
- Japanese tissue paper (optional), cut to 8½ inches (21.6 cm) long and 3 inches (7.6 cm) wide
- Ribbon for bookmark, ¼–⅜ inch (6–10 mm) wide
- Endbands (see page 137 for options)
- 1 sheet of book board, at least 8¾ x 11 inches (22.2 x 27.9 cm), 0.08 inch (2 mm), short grain
- 1 strip of 1 x 8¾ inch (2.5 x 22.2 cm) card stock paper, 80–100lb (216–270gsm) cover weight, grain long
- 1 sheet of 11 x 15 inch (27.9 x 38.1 cm) book cloth for the covers
- Moisture barrier sheets

## tools

- Bone folder
- Ruler
- Pencil
- Awl
- Scissors
- Needle
- Glue brush
- Pressing equipment: book press, clamps or weights
- Cutting mat
- Utility knife
- Medium hammer with a slightly rounded face (e.g., cobbler's hammer or mallet)
- Artist or washi tape
- ¼-inch (6-mm) spacer
- ¾-inch (1.9-cm) spacer
- Rotary cutter

## Making the Text Block

In this project, the signature count has been increased to ensure adequate spine swell for rounding. Using a slightly thicker thread can also increase spine swell. The text block should have a wedge shape after it's sewn.

I.   Start by folding four sheets of writing paper in half, with the short edges meeting each other. Crease the fold with the bone folder. Flip the folded papers vertically and crease the fold one more time. This is the first signature, which should measure 5½ x 8½ inches (14 x 21.6 cm). Make twelve more signatures like this.

2.   Follow the instructions for the French Link Stitch (page 46), steps 3 through 21 for sewing the text block. Throughout those steps, you will be using the strip of stiff paper, ruler, pencil, awl, thread, scissors and needle.

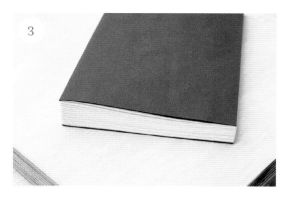

3.  Fold the two endpaper sheets in half one at a time with the smooth or patterned side on the inside and crease the fold with the bone folder. Use a waste sheet with a straight edge to mask the first endpaper, leaving a narrow strip, about ⅛ inch (3 mm), at the fold. Use your glue brush to apply PVA glue to the exposed narrow strip. Tip in the endpaper to one side of the text block, lining up the folded edges without exceeding the signature. Press along the glued edge to adhere. Tip in the remaining endpaper onto the other side of the text block.

## Gluing the Spine

The text block spine only needs to be pressed enough to close the spaces between the signatures. It's important to not press the text block too tightly. To prepare for rounding, glue is applied to the spine, then shaped with a hammer while the glue is still malleable but dry.

4.  Place the text block in between two scrap book boards with the taped edges lined up with the spine. The taped edges will prevent the text block from sticking to the boards. Tap the text block and board sandwich on the desk to bring the signatures to alignment along the spine.

5.  Gluing the spine is easiest if the text block is pressed and propped up vertically with the spine facing up. Apply consistent pressing force on the signature folds along the spine. Here are a few ways you can press the spine.

• If you have a book press, slide the sandwiched text block into the press with ¼ inch (6 mm) of the spine edge extending beyond the edge of the press. Press the text block and lift the press to stand vertically.

• Using spring clamps or C-clamps, press the sandwiched text block, making sure there is light, even pressure along the spine. Avoid pinching any part of the spine and over-tightening the clamps. Prop up the text block between two boxy weights to stand (image 5).

• The text block can be pressed under weights as it lays horizontally. Place the sandwiched text block in between two boxy weights, such as heavy books. Have ¼ inch (6 mm) of the spine edge extend beyond the weights so that you can work on the spine. Use stable weights to prevent shifting.

Note: When pressing the text block, aim to align the signatures at the head and tail as best as possible for smooth and level edges.

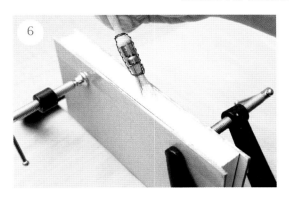

6. Cut the thread ends down to about ¼ inch (6 mm). Brush a generous layer of PVA glue along the length of the spine, but not so much that it pools and seeps in between the signatures. Using an awl or the tip of the brush handle, tuck the thread ends in between the signatures. Use the tip of the brush to stipple glue over the links or use your fingers to push glue into hard-to-reach areas. Cover all the gaps in the spine and let the glue dry to touch.

> Tip: Run the tip of the awl between the outer signatures and the pressing boards to remove glue for easier detaching later.

7. Take the book out of the press. Slowly detach the pressing boards from the text block and remove any excess dried glue. The fore edge can be trimmed at this step, but it's optional since the text block is quite thick. The book in the photos was not trimmed. As the text block is rounded in the next step, the fore edge will become a concave edge.

## Rounding the Spine

A rounded spine is not only aesthetically pleasing, but it also allows bookbinders to make thicker books that hold up over time. Rounding reduces spine swell, which levels out the text block and prevents the spine from collapsing or slumping when opened.

Before the glue has fully set, the spine can be shaped and rounded. Use a medium-sized hammer with a slightly rounded smooth face, such as a cobbler's hammer or mallet. A flat face with sharp edges can easily cause nicks. As you feel the paper respond to the hammering, you can adjust the force of your hits. Too much force can damage the folds. Aim for an evenly rounded arch, about ⅓ of a circle, with no flat spots or peaks.

> Note: Rounding is often followed by backing, which is the forming of square shoulders for the book boards to be connected. This prevents the pages from sagging as the book sits upright on a shelf over time. Backing requires advanced equipment like angled backing boards or irons and a finishing press, so we will only be rounding the text block in this project.

8. To set up for rounding, place the text block on a sturdy surface with the spine facing away from you. With your non-dominant hand, position your thumb on the fore edge and your fingers on top. Pull the top signatures towards you by gripping your fingers as you press your thumb against the fore edge. This pulling motion slopes the spine and exposes the top signatures for hammering.

9. Hammer down at a slight angle, starting at the mid-spine and move towards the head and tail with gentle, sweeping blows. You can either sweep downwards or upwards as you strike. Hammering downwards along the spine edge helps compress the spine. Hammering upwards shapes the spine quickly, but it can be easy to overdo it. After working the whole length of the spine, flip the book and round the other side. Work up and down the spine two to three times on one side before turning it over to work on the other side.

10. Look at the head and tail frequently to check your rounding progress. Check the fore edge as well, to see that the concave shape is developing evenly. Keep hammering on either side of the spine as many times as you need to achieve an arch resembling one-third of a circle. The spine thickness should now be level with the fore edge.

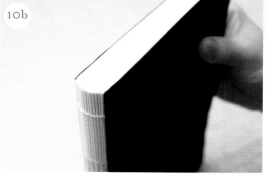

Tip: When finished, check the consistency of the rounding by wrapping a strip of paper around the spine and marking the spine width at the head, mid-spine, and tail. Measure and write down all three widths, which should have no more than ¹⁄₃₂–¹⁄₁₆-inch (1–2-mm) difference. Make minor adjustments if necessary. A consistent, well-rounded spine will have good structural support to enable spine movement.

## Lining the Spine

A rounded spine is lined with support and decorative materials just like a flat spine. The linings should be pressed firmly onto the spine for full adhesion.

11. Place the book back into the press, with the spine extending beyond the edge of the pressing boards, about ½ inch (1.3 cm).

Note: I prefer to line the spine while the text block is propped upright, but this is not necessary. You can work on the spine on lifted platforms as it lies flat.

12. Confirm that the strip of mull is the same length as the spine. Brush on a thin layer of glue along the length of the spine. Center the mull onto the spine and lay it on. Press firmly with your fingers to adhere and rub on with the bone folder. It's important for the mull to be attached fully, forming over the round and all the little bumps on the spine, so that the mull can do its job of supporting spine movement.

Tip: If you prefer extra spine support, add another layer of thin, Japanese tissue paper. The long kozo fibers of the paper offer a good amount of hold without adding any bulk to the spine.

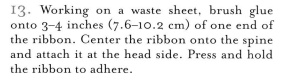

13. Working on a waste sheet, brush glue onto 3–4 inches (7.6–10.2 cm) of one end of the ribbon. Center the ribbon onto the spine and attach it at the head side. Press and hold the ribbon to adhere.

14. Brush glue onto one endband, avoiding the piping, and stipple glue onto the text block and ribbon, being careful to not get glue on the part of the ribbon that will be visible beyond the text block. Attach the endband onto the text block. Press and hold to adhere. Glue on the remaining endband.

15. Carefully remove the text block from the press. Measure out the ribbon to be at least 3 inches (7.6 cm) longer than the length of the book and trim it with scissors. Slip the ribbon bookmark into the middle of the text block, leaving some slack at the top so the adhesive is not disturbed. Confirm that all of the spine linings are adhered and set the text block aside to dry.

Note: Some bookbinders prefer to add an additional support mechanism called an Oxford hollow, which is intended to help the spine break away from the text block when the book is open. It's a tri-fold piece of paper formed into a hollow tube, then attached onto the spine of the text block and the cover.

## Making the Hardcover Case

The spine of the case will be made of card stock paper, which is rounded to hug the spine of the text block.

16. Let's start by making the front and back covers. Measure and write down the width and length of the endpapers. The cover boards will be the same width as the endpaper, but the length will be that of the spine plus ¼ inch (6 mm). The additional spacing creates a cover overhang of ⅛ inch (3 mm) at the head and tail. Cut two pieces of book board, with the grain running parallel to the spine. Hold the boards against the text block to confirm that the width is the same as the endpaper and that the length extends beyond the text block ⅛ inch (3 mm) at the head and tail.

17a

17b

17. To make the spine stiffener, measure the width by wrapping a strip of paper around the spine. Mark the width at the head, mid-spine, and tail. Take the widest measurement for the width of the spine stiffener. The length is the same as the cover boards. Cut a piece of card stock according to these measurements, with the paper grain running lengthwise, parallel to the spine. The paper grain will allow the spine stiffener to round easily.

18

## Test Fitting the Hardcover Case

18. One of the common measurement errors for this project is having covers that are too short or long compared to the text block. Here is one way to check that the boards are the right size before committing to covering the boards. To test the fit of the case, use two pieces of artist tape, about 5 inches (12.7 cm), and place them horizontally across the spine stiffener. Flip the spine over and place a ¼-inch (6-mm) spacer on one side, against the spine stiffener. Then place a cover board against the spacer, checking for alignment at the head and tail. Move the spacer to the other side of the spine board and place the remaining cover board. Remove the spacer and wrap the boards around the text block. Push the text block firmly into the inner spine and center it between the head and tail, pulling the covers outward to maximize the hinge gap. The hinge gap may seem roomy now, but once the cover material is applied, the hinge will be stabilized. Check that there is an even overhang trim, about ⅛ inch (3 mm) around the head, tail and fore edge. The fore edge is likely to be too long. With a pencil, mark where the text block fore edge ends on the cover boards. Measure and mark ⅛ inch (3 mm) past this mark to indicate the cover overhang. Make the same marks on the opposite cover and, with your ruler and utility knife, trim both boards to size. Trim any other part of the case to your liking and test fit the case after each adjustment. Note that the book cloth will add some bulk to all sides of the cover.

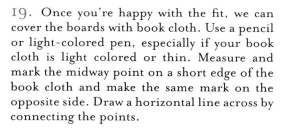

19. Once you're happy with the fit, we can cover the boards with book cloth. Use a pencil or light-colored pen, especially if your book cloth is light colored or thin. Measure and mark the midway point on a short edge of the book cloth and make the same mark on the opposite side. Draw a horizontal line across by connecting the points.

20. Measure and mark the midway point on a long edge of the book cloth and make the same mark on the opposite side. Draw a vertical midline by connecting the points. These lines will be helpful for centering and squaring the boards.

21. Brush a thin layer of glue onto the spine stiffener. Attach it squarely onto the center of the book cloth, using the midlines as guides.

22. Place a ¼-inch (6-mm) spacer on the right side of the spine board. Brush a thin layer of glue onto a cover board and attach it against the spacer, making sure the spine and cover boards line up at the head and tail. Press firmly to adhere.

23. Place a ¼-inch (6-mm) spacer on the left side of the spine board. Brush a thin layer of glue onto the remaining cover board and attach it against the spacer, making sure the spine and cover boards line up at the head and tail. Press firmly to adhere.

24. Flip the cover over and rub on the book cloth with the long edge of the bone folder with medium pressure. Smooth from the center moving outward. Score the hinges by digging the tip of the bone folder into the hinge gaps, pressing along the edges of the boards.

25. Flip the cover over. Trim each edge of the book cloth with a ¾-inch (1.9-cm) spacer and rotary cutter. Cut each corner of the decorative paper at a 45-degree angle, leaving about ⅛ inch (3 mm) of excess.

26. Starting at the top edge of the cover, brush a thin layer of glue onto the tab of book cloth. Wrap the tab around the board, flatten at the spine stiffener, and press firmly throughout. Smooth out the glued tab with a bone folder. Repeat for the tab on the opposite side of this cover. Press the book cloth into the hinge gap with the bone folder.

27. Let's turn in the side tabs. Brush glue onto one of the remaining two tabs. Use the bone folder to tuck in and press the corner bits flat. Wrap the tab over the book board's edge. Repeat for the last side tab.

28. Slightly round the spine stiffener by holding the cover boards with each hand and rubbing the inner spine against a straight table edge. Round it further by gently pressing the width along the spine stiffener.

The case is complete! Lay the cover flat to dry, at least 20 minutes. You can also lightly press it under weights to flatten it while it dries. It is normal if the covers bow out slightly when they're dry. Gluing the endpapers to the inner covers will "pull" the cover inward to straighten them out. The goal is to find a balance between the pulling forces of the different materials glued onto the outer and inner covers.

29. To case in the text block and complete the book, follow steps 24 through 28 in Case Binding (page 139). Casing in a rounded spine book is the same method as a flat spine. Make sure that the text block spine is pressed snugly into the spine stiffener throughout the process. Score the hinge with the bone folder against the cover board edge for a more pronounced hinge.

Congratulations on making a rounded spine book! You've come a long way.

design your own book

The projects have set dimensions, but once you've become familiar with them and discover some of your favorite bindings, you can adapt the instructions to make books of any size and change up the materials. Here are some steps you can take to come up with a design for your book.

1.    What is the purpose of the book? Knowing how the book will be used will help you decide everything else.

2.    Select a book structure that has the features you need. For example, the book may need pages that open flat (Coptic Stitch Binding, page 94), have spacing between the signatures for photos or ephemera (Long Stitch Binding, page 110) or have a sturdy flatback spine (Case Binding, page 138).

3.    Decide the type of paper that you will be using for the pages, as well as the desired page count. Sketch out a plan with measurements.

4.    Create your own punching guide. The outer kettle stitches should generally be ½ to ¾ inch (1.3 to 1.9 cm) from the head and tail and the stitches in between should be evenly distributed along the spine to offer adequate support.

5.    Choose the cover materials that inspire you. For structures that have spine boards or spine stiffeners, use book cloth for the hinges for durability. If you wish to use decorative paper along with book cloth, apply the materials with quarter binding (page 111).

I recommend practicing your favorite binding many times to improve your skills and understanding. Don't fret if your books aren't perfect or beautiful; each wonky book represents a step in your bookbinding journey. I hope you find a great deal of enjoyment and satisfaction in creating your own book designs and finding your personal bookbinding style.

# finishing touches

I'm excited to share a few of my favorite ways
to customize and add personality to handmade
books inside and out.

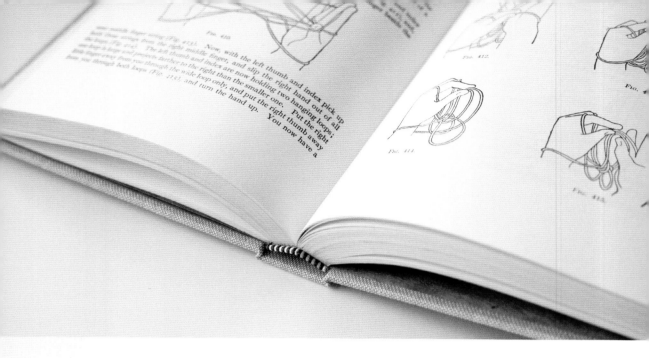

# Adding a Hardcover to a Paperback Book

*Virtually all paperback books published today are perfect bound with a glued spine, including this book that you're holding! You can add a hardcover case to any paperback book to reinforce the spine and protect the pages, or to simply give it a different look. If you have a sentimental novel you'd like to rebind, I recommend practicing on a different similar-sized book to get familiar with the process.*

## materials

- Paperback book
- 2 sheets of endpaper, grain short, at least double the size of the book
- Waste sheets
- PVA glue
- Strip of mull, length of the spine and triple the width of the spine
- Japanese tissue paper (optional), length of the spine and triple the width of the spine
- Ribbon bookmark (optional)
- Endbands
- 2 pieces of scrap book board larger than the book width and length
- Book cloth
- Book board
- Moisture barrier sheets

## tools

- Medium to fine grit sandpaper
- Bone folder
- Metal ruler
- Utility knife
- Glue brush
- Pressing equipment: book press, clamps or weights
- Hinge rods (or double-pointed knitting needles, size 0–2 [2–2.75 mm]) for forming the hinges

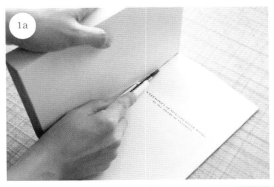

## Prepare the Paperback

Before making the covers, the book needs to be prepared like any other text block.

1. Carefully peel or cut off the front and back covers and the spine of the paperback, leaving the binding intact. If needed, sand the spine with sandpaper to remove the glossy or coated spine layer, and to roughen the surface for attaching spine linings.

2. If the glue binding is brittle and breaking, it will need to be rebound. Even if the break is glued back together, it will remain a weak spot and can easily break again. To rebind the book, trim the spine as narrow as possible to remove the glued edge, with the edge trimming technique described on page 25. Make sure there's adequate gutter margin on the inner pages for trimming. Press and rebind the book following steps 4 through 7 for Perfect Binding (page 38).

3. Prepare two endpaper sheets that are double the size of the book. Fold each sheet in half with the smooth or patterned side on the inside and use the bone folder on the crease. Then use your ruler and utility knife to trim the folded sheets to the same size as the book.

4. Tip in the endpapers at the front and back of the book. Working on a waste sheet, mask the endpaper leaving a narrow strip, about ⅛ inch (3 mm), exposed at the fold. Brush glue onto the exposed endpaper and attach it onto the paperback, lined up at the spine. Repeat for the remaining endpaper.

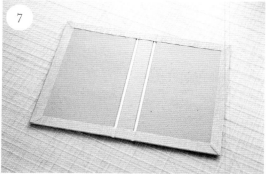

5. Reinforce the spine and hinges with mull. Measure and cut a piece of mull that is the same length as the spine. The mull width should be about three times the width of the spine, or 2 inches (5 cm) wider than the spine, whichever is smaller. Brush a thin layer of glue onto the book spine and center the mull. Press with your fingers or bone folder to ensure it's adequately glued along the whole spine.

6. If you prefer, glue on a ribbon bookmark at the head edge of the spine. The ribbon should be glued onto about one-third of the spine length. Attach endbands at the head and tail of the spine with glue as well.

## Make the Hardcover Case

7. Follow the instructions for steps 12 through 23 in Case Binding (page 139) to create a hardcover case, but with the following modification of the hinge gap: Since this book will be read and does not need to lay as flat as a writing journal, the hinge space will be ¼ inch (6 mm). Be sure to test fit the case against the text block and trim the boards to the desired size.

8. Using the test fitted hardcover case as a guide, measure and cut book cloth that is 2 inches longer and wider than the boards.

9. Continue to follow instructions for casing in the text block, steps 24 through 28, starting on page 146.

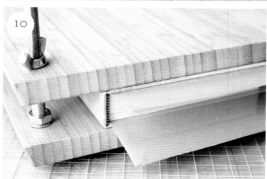

## Press the Book

10. Place moisture barrier sheets in the inner covers, then press the book using a book press or placing it under heavy stable weights. Use hinge rods if you'd like to form visible shoulders. Keep the book in the press for at least eight hours (or overnight) to dry.

11. Remove the book from the press and warm up the spine by opening the book in the middle first, then the first ⅓ of the book, and finally the last ⅓ of the book. Open the front and back covers to examine the endpapers.

The book is complete! If you would like to add a title to the book, I suggest attaching a printed title card onto the cover with PVA glue. Talk to your local letterpress printer before you make the book to see if they can help you print titles into the covers. They may have recommendations for cover materials that are suitable for printing.

## Securing the Book with Closures

- - - - - - - - - - - - - - - - - - - - - - - - - - - - - - - - - - - - - - - -

*Closures don't only keep a book closed; they also help maintain the binding, protect the pages and keep*
*loose contents within the book. Here are some ways you can add closures to your handmade book.*

- - - - - - - - - - - - - - - - - - - - - - - - - - - - - - - - - - - - - - - -

Sew your own **journal band** with fold-over elastic (image 1). Measure elastic by wrapping it around the book, then cut it to the desired length. Seal the edges with a lighter to prevent fraying. Add a pen loop before closing the band. Elastic journal bands are suitable for any hardcover book.

1

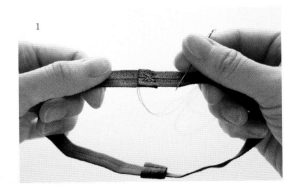

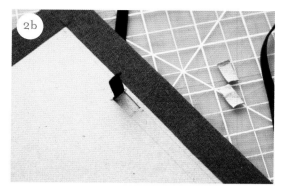

To create a book with an **embedded band** (image 2a), the elastic is installed into the covers before the endpapers are attached or before the text block is cased in. A common material used is knit elastic. On the back cover, decide where the two ends should be attached. Cut a slit, slightly wider than the elastic band, into the cover with the utility knife or a small chisel (image 2b). The slits should be at least ½ inch (1.3 cm) from the edge. On the inner cover, create a ½-inch (1.3-cm) grave for the elastic end to be glued into so that it will be flush with the board. Push the elastic end through with an awl and attach it with PVA glue. The attachment will be hidden under the endpapers. Complete your book with the rest of the bookbinding process and press the book.

**Ribbon ties** (image 3a) add an elegant accent to any book. They can be easily sewn into fabric soft covers. For hardcovers, the ribbon can be attached securely with the embedding method described above, or it can be attached after the book is completed. Cut a slit, slightly wider than the ribbon, into the cover with the utility knife or a small chisel (image 3b). The slits should be at least ½ inch (1.3 cm) from the edge. Push the ribbon through with an awl and attach ½ inch (1.3 cm) of the end with PVA glue. Secure the ribbon by gluing on a rectangle piece of paper that's the same color as the endpapers (image 3c). The paper should cover ¼ inch (6 mm) on each side of the ribbon. Alternatively, you can use hot glue as a secure adhesive to attach ribbon onto the inner cover without cutting a slit into the cover.

4a

4b

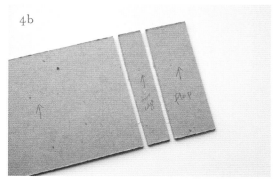

Create a **hinged fore edge flap with a magnet closure** (image 4a). While constructing the case, add two more pieces of board next to the back cover, spaced ¼ inch (6 mm) apart (image 4b). The fore-edge piece is the width of the spine board plus the thickness of one board and the outermost piece should be a quarter width of the cover. Cut and peel the board to create graves to hold magnets and seal it in with tissue paper (image 4c). Cover the boards with book cloth and score the spaces between the boards with the bone folder (image 4d). Press the completed book with the fore edge flap open.

For fabric covers, such as the one in Long Stitch with Wrap-Around Cover (page 56), head to the sewing store to see the kinds of closures available, such as **snap buttons** and **velcro fasteners**. Hand-sew the closures onto the fabric or use an extra strong glue.

4c

4d

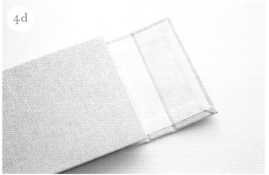

# Fun and Functional Pockets

- - - - - - - - - - - - - - - - - - - - - - - - - - - - - - - - - - - - - - - - - - - -

*If you're a collector of sentimental keepsakes, you may enjoy having pockets in your book. They can be added to the inner covers or be a part of the text block. Use a stiff and sturdy material like card stock and a strong wet glue like PVA.*

- - - - - - - - - - - - - - - - - - - - - - - - - - - - - - - - - - - - - - - - - - - -

To make **simple add-on pockets**, measure the spacing of where the pocket will go and decide the shape of the pocket. Draw out the pocket with dimensions on a notepad, adding ½ inch (1.3 cm) tabs at the bottom and side(s) of the pocket (image 1a). Cut a piece of card stock paper, then score and fold the tabs with the bone folder. Then trim each corner at a 45-degree angle (image 1b). Brush glue onto the tabs and position the pocket. Press with a weight.

1a

1b

1c

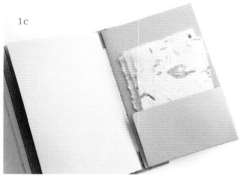

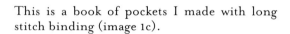

2a

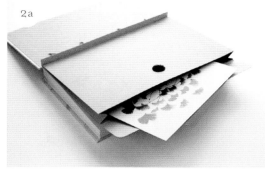

2b

2c

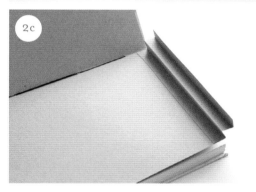

This is a book of pockets I made with long stitch binding (image 1c).

To make an **expandable pocket** (image 2a) in the text block, sew a card stock folio as one of the signatures. Cut two strips of card stock paper that measure the width of the folio by 2 inches (5 cm), with the grain running lengthwise for easy folding. Fold the two strips into accordions with three folds (image 2b). Use the bone folder to make crisp folds. Cut another strip of paper that measures the length of the folio by 2 inches (5 cm), grain long. This will be the flap. When the book is complete, glue the accordions and the flap on the inside of the card stock folio with PVA glue (image 2c). Fold the flap over and press to flatten. Add a Velcro fastener to keep the flap closed.

Use **pre-made pockets and envelopes** as a quick and easy method such as a library pocket (image 3). If you want to prevent paper wrinkling from moisture, use double-sided tape as the adhesive.

3

# important things to know

## Paper Sizes

North America has their own system of paper sizing, and in the rest of the world, the A-series is widespread. Understanding the available paper sizes helps us determine the size of books we can make. Here's a quick reference guide to the sizes.

### North American Sizes

**Letter:** 8½ x 11 inches (216 x 279 mm)

**Legal:** 8½ x 14 inches (216 x 356 mm)

**Tabloid/Ledger:** 11 x 17 inches (279 x 432 mm)

**Arch A:** 9 x 12 inches (229 x 305 mm)

**Arch B:** 12 x 18 inches (305 x 457 mm)

"Arch" refers to the architectural paper series, a common size used for fine art papers.

### International Sizes

**A3:** 11.7 x 16.5 inches (297 x 420 mm)

**A4:** 8.3 x 11.7 inches (210 x 297 mm)

**A5:** 5.8 x 8.3 inches (148 x 210 mm)

**A6:** 4.1 x 5.8 inches (105 x 148 mm)

## Common Notebook Sizes

Major stationery companies have set standards for notebook sizes that we've become familiar with. You'll find that blank books vary a lot in size, but these are a few of the common ones. Since A4 paper has similar dimensions to letter size paper, we can refer to a notebook made with letter size paper folded in half as an A5 book.

**A4 large:** Tabloid or A3 paper folded in half

**A5 standard:** Letter or A4 paper folded in half

**A6 pocket:** Letter or A4 paper cut in half widthwise, then folded in half

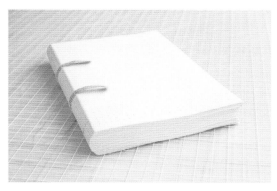

## Managing Spine Swell

Spine swell is the expanded thickness of the text block spine after it's sewn. Thread adds bulk, so it's important to use the right thread gauge for your project. The goal is to achieve level text blocks from spine to fore edge when the book is complete. Use a thread such as $^{25}/_3$ gauge or thinner. The signatures can also be pressed before they're sewn for extra flattening. Generally, make text blocks that are no thicker than ¾ inch (2 cm) for minimum swell. Successful spine swell control results in the best looking and functioning books.

If the text block has a wedge shape, the spine can be rounded to reduce the swell. You may want to intentionally increase spine swell when constructing the text block to make a rounded spine book. Choose to increase the number of signatures or use slightly thicker thread for added bulk. The acceptable amount of swell is up to 30 percent for rounding. Rounding a spine is both a structural and aesthetic choice. See page 158 for instructions on making a rounded spine book.

Too much swell can cause the spine to slope or slump, creating a weak spot in the structure. However, if you make a book that has spine swell and it functions well, that's perfectly fine.

To **minimize** spine swell, use thinner thread, fold more sheets per signature and/or sew fewer signatures.

To **increase** spine swell, use thicker thread, fold fewer sheets per signature and/or sew more signatures.

Note: Heavier books with a lot of swell require backing in addition to rounding. Backing involves pressing the text block between angled boards and the rounded spine is continually hammered until 90-degree shoulders form at the hinges where the cover boards are attached. This is an advanced technique that requires backing boards or irons, a finishing press and a bookbinding hammer.

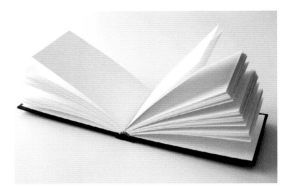

## Spines that Breathe

A flexible and strong book spine is important for the user's experience and the longevity of the book. While a lay-flat feature is preferred for blank page books, it's actually difficult to make a durable book that can truly lay flat, with the exception of some exposed spine bindings. Hardcover case bound books naturally have a gutter, which is the inner margin space between the pages when the book is open. There are ways to construct the book to optimize flexibility in the spine and hinges, so that the book can reach its full range of movement. The following suggestions are suitable for beginner case bindings.

The sewing method, spine linings and hinges affect spine movement. To make hardcover books that lay as flat as possible, use a strong sewing method, such as French Link Stitch (page 46). Use minimal spine linings without compromising the strength. Mull is the minimum required lining material to support the text block spine. Use a thin, flexible endband that doesn't add bulk or restrict the movement of the spine. If possible, source mull and endbands from a bookbinding supply shop to ensure you're using good quality materials. A slightly wider hinge gap can also aid in covers opening more easily. For standard case bindings, I prefer to use a ⅜-inch (1-cm) hinge gap for journals and sketchbooks. Feel free to experiment with different hinge gap widths.

The size and weight of the pages can also help with keeping the book open. The wider and heavier the pages, the more drape there is on either side of the spine, weighing the covers down.

# troubleshooting common mistakes

While bookbinding is a very satisfying craft, it can also be frustrating at times! In the beginning, I didn't understand why certain issues were happening and kept happening. With so many steps in making a book, there's bound to be mistakes made, and that's okay. Each mistake is a building block towards making really great books. My general advice is to make one book repeatedly as a study of the book structure and its subtleties. Your abilities and skills will surely grow with practice! Here are a few common mistakes that I've had to troubleshoot.

## Sewing Too Tight or Loose

Sewing that is too tight can cause the pages to open stiffly and awkwardly. Loose sewing will cause the signatures to shift and easily come out of alignment. With your first books, it's normal to sew too tightly or loosely.

It's important to use the right thread and needle gauge that will add the least amount of bulk at the spine. Spine swell can cause the signatures to slope and misalign. Start with a standard thread gauge, such as $^{25}/_3$, and punch holes that are just big enough for the tip of your needle to pierce through. Large holes can lead to loose and uneven sewing as well.

To sew with the right thread tension, pull taut (not tight) at each stitch and at the end of each signature. Pulling taut involves removing slack in the thread but not tightening further than that. Be gentle when pulling on the thread, and pull towards the direction that you're sewing, parallel to the signature folds. If you pull backwards or in another direction, you risk tearing the signature. In this case, you can tape the tear and continue sewing or replace the signature altogether. There will be times when thread tension needs to be slightly tighter, such as exposed spine bindings that solely rely on the stitching for spine support.

Sewn text blocks will naturally be a little loose and will shift between the signatures before they are glued and reinforced. This looseness allows bindings like Coptic stitch to lay flat. Use waxed thread to better hold signatures together and tie effective knots. With practice, sewing with the right amount of tension will come with muscle memory.

## Too Much or Too Little Glue

It can get messy quickly when it's time to add glue to your book! Wet waste sheets with glue residue piling up and sticky, gluey fingers touching everything was a recurring experience of mine. Pasting paper with the right amount of glue within a short time period takes some practice. Using too much glue can cause unwanted oozing and seeping to other parts of the book. If the spine feels too stiff, there may have been glue that crept into the spine or hinges from pressing. Too much glue can also cause wrinkling and tearing from the wetness. When insufficient glue is applied, the glue can dry before attaching material, causing inconsistent adhesion and air bubbles.

To apply the right amount of glue, use a glue brush that is proportional to the size of your piece of paper and source a quality PVA glue. Bookbinding PVA glue has a viscosity somewhere between honey and maple syrup. Thin glue may be too wet, and thick glue may be difficult to spread evenly. It's generally better to brush glue onto the heavier paper since lighter papers are more likely to expand.

Being prepared with clean tools, waste sheets, moisture barrier sheets and a wet cloth can help you stay organized. Knowing your workflow and accessing the necessary materials for gluing allows you to move quickly and decisively.

## Fixing Bowing Covers

Even after you've compensated for paper pull and pressed the book adequately, you may still find yourself with cover boards that bow outward. Here are some solutions to try for straightening out the covers.

For exposed sewing bindings, glue another endpaper sheet of the same size to the inner cover. Insert moisture barrier sheets to protect the pages and press the book under weights to dry. The moisture will seep through to the board and the additional sheet will provide some inward pulling force. Alternatively, you can slowly remove the endpaper with a blade to expose the board. Glue on a light- or medium-weight paper within the turn-ins, then glue a new sheet of endpaper on top.

For case bindings, remove the text block to work on the case. Carefully cut out the text block at the hinges of the inner cover without damaging the case. Reprepare the text block by replacing the endpapers and applying another layer of mull. To treat the case, tear off the remaining endpaper as evenly as possible. Glue a thin piece of paper onto the inner cover within the turn-ins. Let the case dry under weights. Check the case when it's dry. Did the bowing reduce? It's acceptable that slight bowing remains because it should straighten out when the text block is cased in.

For covers that bow inwards, the grain of the endpaper may be running across rather than parallel to the spine, which pulls on the head and tail of the cover. Carefully cut out the text block and peel off the endpaper as much as you can. Reattach endpaper with the correct paper grain. If the endpaper grain is correct, paper will need to be glued onto the front of the board to compensate the pull. Depending on the book structure, this may mean that you will need to undo the binding to re-cover the board or tear off the book cloth to reconstruct the case.

Dealing with bowing covers is part of the process, even for professional bookbinders. It can often happen when you're working with a new material that you're unfamiliar with. Personally, I keep and use all of my books that have bowing covers since they're still perfectly good books!

## Misalignments and Wrong Measurements

I've made countless wonky, lopsided books in my bookbinding practice. It's often a result of miscalculating a measurement or not considering how a small measurement will affect the final outcome. Getting the measurements right is key to making professional-looking books!

Here are five tips for minimizing measurement errors:

1. Double check every measurement and confirm that the corners are square before making a cut.

2. Start with simple structures. There is less measuring involved, which can help you gain confidence for more complex bindings.

3. Sketch and write out the measurements of your project. This will help you keep track of proportions and easily make adjustments. The template will also be useful for the next time you make it.

4. Test fit pieces before you glue. This can save you from trying to fix a mismeasurement after papers are adhered.

5. Take note of the proportions of book components. This can help you create a book that feels "just right." Start with standard- or medium-sized book projects and decide your preferences for board thickness, decorative material weight, paper weight, spine thickness, hinge gaps and more.

As you make more books, you'll notice patterns and come up with your own measuring tricks. Measuring will feel habitual, and your eye for accuracy will develop!

# make your own book press

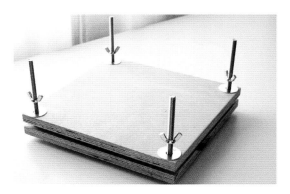

A book press can be very helpful for applying controlled and consistent pressure at various stages of making a book. I use it most often to glue and line text block spines, as well as in the final stage of setting hardcover books to dry. The pressure allows nice shoulders or grooves to form with hinge rods, or in my case, double-pointed knitting needles.

Wooden book presses can be costly and hard to find, but it's straightforward to make one at home, if you or someone you know can drill holes into wood. Hardware stores that sell lumber can typically make free or cheap custom cuts. Consider the size of books you'd like to make when mocking up the build plan. The following instructions are my suggestion for building your own press to make books under 10 inches (25.4 cm) long.

## materials

- 2 sheets (12 x 12 inch [30.5 x 30.5 cm]) of quality plywood ½–¾ inch (1.3–1.9 cm) thick, sanded and finished
- 4 (⅜ x 6–inch [1 x 15.2–cm]) full thread hex bolts
- 4 (⅜–inch [1–cm]) lock washers
- 4 (⅜–inch [1–cm]) nuts
- 4 (⅜–inch [1–cm]) flat washers
- 4 (⅜–inch [1–cm]) wing nuts
- 4 screw-on rubber bumper feet

## tools

- Power drill with ⅜–inch (1–cm) and ½–inch (1.3–cm) drill bits
- Wood clamps such as C-clamps

Tip: Instead of lumber, use cutting boards!

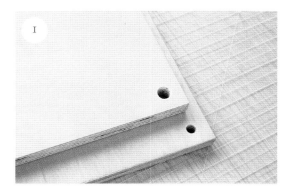

Check that the plywood is not warped and has smooth, flat surfaces. Clamp both boards firmly together, with the edges flush. Mark ¾ inch (1.9 cm) from each corner towards the center. Drill ⅜-inch (1-cm) holes through both boards at the same time, and then remove the clamps to separate the boards.

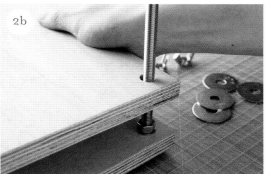

1.  With the top board only, redrill the holes with a ½-inch (1.3-cm) drill bit to create space for raising and lowering the press. Sand down any rough areas.

2.  Screw the bolts upwards into the bottom board and secure them with washers and nuts. Then thread the top board through the bolts and screw on the wing nuts. You may need to redrill the holes if it feels too tight when raising and lowering the top board.

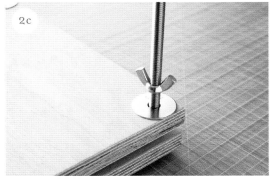

3.  Install the rubber feet on the bottom of the press.

# resources and references

If you ever get the chance to take a workshop or course in bookbinding, I highly recommend it. Look for a book arts center in your city or non-profit organizations that are dedicated to keeping the craft alive. These organizations often have local chapters offering learning opportunities and resources listed on their website.

**Here are a few organizations to check out**

- Canadian Bookbinders and Book Artists Guild
- Guild of Book Workers (U.S.)
- Society of Bookbinders (U.K.)

**For bookbinding supplies, I recommend these online shops based in the U.S.**

- Book Craft Supply
- Colophon Book Arts
- Hiromi Paper
- Hollander's
- Mulberry Paper and More
- Paperworks
- TALAS
- The Paper Mill Store

**Here is a list of references I used while writing this book**

- Conroy, T. (1987). *The Movement of the Book Spine*. The American Institute for Conservation. https://cool.culturalheritage.org/coolaic/sg/bpg/annual/v06/bp06-01.html
- Cowie, B. (2018). *Grain Direction – The Long and Short of It*. PostPress. https://postpressmag.com/articles/2018/grain-direction-the-long-and-short-of-it/
- Gee, D. (2015). *Japanese Bookbinding*. American Bookbinders Museum. https://bookbindersmuseum.org/japanese-bookbinding/
- *Glossary of Binding Terms*. (1996). The Book Arts Web. https://www.philobiblon.com/gbwarticle/bindterm.htm
- Hanmer, K. (2013). *Variations on the Drum Leaf and Sewn Boards Bindings*. Guild of Book Workers. https://guildofbookworkers.org/sites/default/files/standards/2013_gbw_drum_sewn_hanmer-1.pdf
- *History of Suminagashi and Marbling*. (2017). Suminagashi. https://suminagashi.com/history/
- The Library of Congress. (n.d.). *The Deterioration and Preservation of Paper: Some Essential Facts*. https://www.loc.gov/preservation/care/deterioratebrochure.html
- Verheyen, P. D. (2009). *Der Gebrochene Rücken: A variation of the German case binding*. Walpole, NH: Hedi Kyle, Festschrift 2009. https://works.bepress.com/peter_verheyen/1/

# acknowledgments

- - - - - - - - - - - - - - - - - - - - - - - - - - - - - - - - - - - - - - - - - - - - - -

Much love to Eli and Lucy for being with me every step of the way, and to Emily for believing in me. Thanks to my family for giving me my creative bones.

I'm grateful to my first ever bookbinding teacher, Suzan Lee, and WePress Community Arts Space for helping me grow as an artist and a teacher.

Huge thanks to my patrons for giving me the time to write and for cheering me on.

I want to acknowledge Jennifer from Sea Lemon, Darryn from DAS Bookbinding and Misty from papercraftpanda, whose content has helped me and so many others deepen our appreciation for bookbinding.

Thank you, Lex, for the beautiful photos; Alexandra, my editor, for her enthusiastic and consistent support; and everyone on the Page Street team for making this book come to life.

# about the author

- - - - - - - - - - - - - - - - - - - - - - - - - - - - - - - - - - - - - - - - - - - - - -

**Chanel Ly** is a bookbinder from Vancouver, BC, the unceded territories of the Musqueam, Squamish and Tsleil-Waututh Peoples. Coming from a family of Chinese-Vietnamese immigrants and a long lineage of creative women deeply informs her artistic voice. She makes books in her cozy home studio with the company of her dog, Lucy. She enjoys documenting her process and sharing calming videos online. Find her as @bittermelonbindery on all platforms.

# index